BIRKET FOSTER

From a photograph by Messrs. C. E. Fry & Son.

BIRKET FOSTER

R.W.S.

BY

H. M. CUNDALL, I.S.O., F.S.A.

BRACKEN BOOKS
LONDON

First published in 1906
by Adam & Charles Black,
London.

This edition published 1986 by Bracken Books,
a division of Bestseller Publications Ltd, Brent House,
24–28 Friern Park, North Finchley, London N12 9DA

ISBN 1 85170 033 1

Printed and bound by Grafoimpex,
Yugoslavia

DEDICATED TO

MYLES BIRKET FOSTER, F.R.A.M.

THE ELDEST SON OF THE ARTIST

LISIEUX.

PREFACE

IT may be asserted without fear of contradiction that the dainty water-colour drawings executed by Birket Foster, of which a large and representative selection are reproduced in this volume, appeal to the majority of the British public more than the works of any other artist.

For many years during the early part of his career he was engaged in drawing on wood-blocks for the engraver, from which he acquired a minuteness in detail that continued to pervade his paintings in later life. The result was that he produced scenes from nature with an exactness that the most uninitiated in art are able to understand and appreciate. The chief features, however, in Birket Foster's paintings are the poetic feeling with which he indued them, and the care and felicity with which his compositions were selected. These qualities lend a great charm to his drawings, and especially to those representing the homely scenes so frequently selected from that picturesque part of Surrey, where he lived for many years. He revelled in sunny landscapes, with sheep roaming in the distance and with rustic children playing in the foreground; he was also attracted by peaceful red-brick cottages covered with thatch, and enlivened by domestic scenes. It is perhaps by these rural paintings that the artist is best known. He, however, wandered far afield in search of the picturesque; he was an indefatigable painter, and produced works selected from all parts of England, Wales, and Scotland. Birket Foster was especially partial to the Northern counties and the district surrounding his native town in Northumberland. His rambles were not confined solely to his own country; he travelled frequently on the Continent; Venice, as well as the Rhine, had its charms for him. The picturesque scenery of Brittany has also been portrayed by his brush, and on one occasion he went as far as Spain and Morocco in pursuit of his art.

Birket Foster was of a most affable and genial disposition, and I have vivid recollections of many of his kindnesses in my younger days, when I lived under my father's roof opposite to the artist's residence in Carlton Hill East. It has afforded me great pleasure to record these few reminiscences of the events in his successful life, and this pleasure has been greatly enhanced by the renewal of a friendship with some members of his family and relatives, of whom I had lost sight for many years owing to our diverging paths in life. I can hardly thank the artist's eldest son, Myles Birket Foster, and the artist's niece, Mrs. Edmund Evans, sufficiently, for all the kind assistance which they have so readily given, not only by placing many of the artist's drawings and sketches at my disposal for the purpose of reproduction, but also by supplying me with many interesting records of his life,

My best thanks are also due to Mr. Robert Dudley for many particulars respecting the artist's method of painting, concerning which Mr. Dudley is well qualified to speak, as he accompanied Birket Foster on several of his tours, and the two artists sketched side by side on many occasions. The details of the dramatic performances at "The Hill," for which Mr. Dudley acted as stage manager at each successive Christmas, have also been supplied by him.

All the illustrations in this volume, excepting the few photographic portraits and views, have been reproduced from original water-colour drawings or pencil sketches, and all these, with the exception of two of the latter by Frederick Walker and one by Charles Keene, were executed by Birket Foster. Some of the sketches in the possession of Mrs. Edmund Evans, and reproduced in the early part of the volume, were drawn at Landells' establishment by Birket Foster when he was only sixteen years of age. These demonstrate the facility with which he could use his pencil even when quite a boy.

The publishers gratefully acknowledge the valuable assistance given by Mr. W. Lockett Agnew in procuring the loan of many of the original paintings for the purpose of illustrating this book, and also the very courteous manner in which Mr. Barnet Lewis, Mr. Sharpley Bainbridge, and Sir Charles Seeley have so readily permitted the finest examples of the artist's works to be selected from their respective collections, and reproductions to be made from them. Sir John D. Milburn, Mr. Jesse Howarth, Mr. Edward Clark, and also the artist's two nieces, Mrs. Alfred Cooper and Mrs. Black, have kindly lent their water-colour drawings by Birket Foster for the same purpose. Lieut. S. B. Boyd-Richardson, R.N., Mr. Sharpley Bainbridge, and Mr. E. G. Cundall have allowed sketches from the artist's note-books in their possession to be reproduced. To all of them the best thanks of the publishers are rendered; also to Miss Evans for her permission to copy the photograph of "The Hill," taken by herself, and to Mr. Croal Thomson for his most obliging aid.

I have also to thank Mr. M. H. Spielmann for kindly giving me information respecting the early designs by Birket Foster executed for *Punch*, and Mr. Algernon Graves for his assistance in the compilation of the list of water-colour drawings exhibited by Birket Foster at the Royal Society of Painters in Water-Colours, of which he was such a distinguished member.

I must add one word of regret. Mrs. Atchison, the artist's only sister, who was looking forward with a lively interest to the appearance of this volume, and who kindly lent one of her brother's earliest water-colour drawings, "The Christmas Holly Cart," for reproduction, did not live to see her wish realised, as she died in her eighty-sixth year, a few days before the publication of the book.

H. M. C.

October 1906.

MANTES, LOOKING SOUTH.

CONTENTS

xiii   *b*

CHARTRES.

LIST OF ILLUSTRATIONS

IN COLOUR

IN BLACK AND WHITE

Ten from Sketches in the possession of Mrs. Edmund Evans (pp. 14, 20, 22, 24, 25, 54, 131, 136, 139).

One from Sketch in the possession of Miss Evans (p. 147).

Thirty-one from Sketch-books in the possession of Lieut. S. B. Boyd-Richardson, R.N. (pp. vii, xiii, xv, 68, 73, 78, 81, 82, 87, 93, 100, 101, 104, 109, 112, 113, 114, 116, 119, 120, 123, 140, 145, 152, 157, 168, 173, 179, 183, 189).

Seven from Sketch-book in the possession of Sharpley Bainbridge, Esq. (pp. 3, 17, 29, 33, 49, 53, 127).

Four from Sketches in the possession of E. G. Cundall, Esq. (pp. 65, 129, 133, 137).

Two from Book-plates (title page and p. 210).

One Birket Foster Monogram as used on his pictures (p. 139).

ETCHING

SHEEP FEEDING . . . . *Preceding the Frontispiece*

From the Original Plate in the possession of H. M. Cundall,
I.S.O., F.S.A.

THE FOSTER FAMILY

CHAPTER I

THE FOSTER FAMILY

BIRKET FOSTER, as he is generally known, or Myles Birket Foster, to give him his full name, was born at North Shields on the 4th February 1825. He was the youngest of seven children, six boys and one girl, all of whom have now passed away.

The name of Myles Birket can be traced back for many generations, and from the pedigree of the Sandys family, which anciently settled at Rathenbury Castle near St Bees, Cumberland, we learn that Esther Sandys of Hawkshead married James, the son of Myles Birket of Birket House, Cartmel, in 1637. Their great-grandson Myles Birket was owner of Hebblethwaite Hall, in the County of York, and Sarthwaite in the County of Lancaster, and his daughter Elizabeth, the sole heiress, married Dodshon Foster, a merchant at Lancaster, who was born in 1730 at Hawthorne, near Sunderland. He was the great-grandson of Robert Foster of Cold Hesledon. In the *Pedigree of the Forsters of Cold Hesledon in the County Palatine of Durham,* written by Joseph Foster in 1862, he states that "the name of Foster is spelt at the beginning of the book Forster, and as the descent is clearly proved by the Registers of the Society of Friends, there is, of course, no doubt that it is correct, but how or why the spelling was changed I have no means of ascertaining."

Dodshon and Elizabeth Foster had one surviving son, Robert, and the following account of his life is extracted from a memoir written by his son and the father of our artist :—

" When about eighteen years old he went to sea, and after making three voyages to the West Indies with Captain Roper in the *Marquis of Rockingham,* he was appointed storekeeper in Antigua by his grandfather and great-uncle, Myles and James Birket, who were then West India merchants."

"About the end of May 1776 he entered on board the brig *Endeavour*, Lieut. Francis Tinsley commander, carrying 4 guns, which was fitted out in Antigua to cruise against the American privateers. On 20th June 1778 he left the *Endeavour* at Spithead and went on board the *Defiance*, 64 guns, Samuel Cranston Goodall, Esq., commander. On 8th July he entered as master's mate on board the *Jupiter*, 50 guns, Francis Reynolds commander. From an entry in his log-book we learn that on 21st October 1778 the *Jupiter* had a severe engagement with the *Triton*, 64 guns. Mr. Roberts, the master, and three men were wounded. Mr. Roberts died the following day, and Robert Foster succeeded him. On 21st April 1779 he received Capt. Reynolds' acting orders as lieutenant of the *Pelican*, 24 guns, Henry Lloyd commander, in the room of Mr. Sumpter deceased."

"In August 1779, his only brother Myles died at Ulverston. In September he obtained leave to visit his friends at Lancaster, which visit brought forth the following letter supposed to have been written by the Vicar of Lancaster :—

Last Sunday, the Quakers at their meeting-house were
thrown into a state of great surprise by the appearance of a
young man in the uniform of a lieutenant of a man-of-war.
This young man's father and grandfather are Quakers, and
being the principal merchants of the place, bred him to the
sea, and afterwards appointed him their storekeeper in the
West Indies, where he was when the American Dispute
began ; and being moved by the spirit (not the peaceable
one of a Quaker, but the true spirit of an Englishman) he
made up his accounts, quitted his store, collected together a
few men from the Lancaster ships, laid aside the Quaker,
mounted a cockade, and joined a Lieutenant Tinsley, then
fitting out a small armed vessel against the Americans, in
which he had several severe actions ; and coming over in her
to Portsmouth, got himself recommended to Captain Reynolds as an officer likely to show him some business, was with
him in the *Jupiter* of 50 guns when they went close alongside the *Triton*, a French 64, at the very time she saw her
consort going off ; and in the heat of that close and desperate
action, on the master being killed, Captain Reynolds immediately sent for Foster from his quarters, and appointed
him master ; and managing the ship for the remainder of
the action, as well as acquitting himself afterwards to the
satisfaction of the captain, upon a vacancy happening lately
at Lisbon, where Captain Reynolds had the command, from
that just and honest principle of rewarding merit Captain
Reynolds deprived himself of a useful officer by appointing
Foster Lieutenant of the *Pelican*.

Foster got leave on the *Pelican* coming to England to
visit his friends at Lancaster for a few days, where he has
withstood all the remonstrances and solicitations to quit the
service, and has gone back to his ship. I hope he will gain
preferment and be a credit to the place, as well as an
example to some others of that society to break through the

principle established by them 'to enjoy all the advantages of peace, but to leave it to others to fight their battles.'

"On his return to Portsmouth the *Pelican* had probably gone to sea without him, as it appears from his log-book that he went on board the *Hornet*, sloop-of-war, 14 guns."

"He remained in the navy a very short time after his visit to Lancaster. His friends, who had been greatly distressed by his desertion from those peaceable principles in which he had been carefully educated, no doubt laboured earnestly while he was with them to induce him to leave the service; and their labours, seconded by his own convictions, seemed to have wrought a wonderful change in the young officer. He became a man of peace, and in after life avoided conversation about his naval career, and certainly never gloried in his former exploits. Soon after he left the navy, his maternal grandfather wanting a manager for his estate near Sedbergh in Yorkshire, which Robert Foster afterwards inherited, he went to reside at Hebblethwaite Hall and settled down as an agriculturist. He erected a mill on the estate for the better employment of the poor, established a school for their education, and became a sort of father, physician, lawyer, and judge among his dependents and country neighbours.   He continued an active, useful, and benevolent life at Hebblethwaite, in the enjoyment of domestic happiness and with social intercourse with the worthies around, who were attracted, by his accomplished mind and genial disposition, to his retired but hospitable dwelling, till the autumn of 1812, when he removed to Newcastle to be near his children, who had most of them removed to that locality.   In 1824 he had a slight attack of paralysis, after which his bodily powers gradually gave way."

The following is an extract from a letter of Robert Southey to Richard Duffa, Esq., on 23th February, 1806, respecting this extraordinary man:—

" Oh, Wordsworth sent me a man the other day, who was worth seeing ; he looked like a first assassin in Macbeth as to his costume—but he was a rare man ; had been a lieutenant in the navy ; was a scholar enough to quote Virgil aptly ; had turned Quaker or semi-Quaker, and was now a dealer in wool somewhere about twenty miles off.   He had seen much and thought much ; his head was well stored, and his heart was in the right place.   It is five- or six-and-twenty years since he was at Lisbon, and he gave me a vivid description of the Belem Convent, as if the impression on his memory was not half a day old.   Edridge's acquaintance, Thomas Wilkinson, came with him.   They had been visiting an old man of a hundred in the vale of Lorton, and it was a fine thing to hear this Robert Foster describe him.   God bless you.   R. S."

Robert Foster married Mary Burton in 1784, and his eldest son, born 4th January 1785 at Hebblethwaite Hall, was named Myles Birket Foster after his maternal great-grandfather, who, was still alive at the time.

Myles Birket Foster married Ann King, who was also a member of a Quaker family, at Newcastle on 11th April 1811, and afterwards went to reside at North Shields, where, as has already been stated, Birket Foster was born.

It will thus be seen that our artist's ancestors held good social positions for many generations in the North Country, and were staunch members of the Society of Friends. One, Sarah Forster, married a descendant of Margaret Fell of Swathmoor Hall, who, after the death of her first husband, Judge Fell, was united to George Fox, the founder of the Quakers.

In 1830 Mr. Foster migrated with his family to London, voyaging all the way by sea. He took up his residence at 40 Charlotte Street, Portland Place, and founded the well-known firm of M. B. Foster and Sons. His youngest son, Birket, was sent to a school kept by two sisters, the Misses F. S. and P. Coar, at Tottenham, and from the letter written from there to his father, of which a facsimile is given, we learn that he received his earliest instruction in drawing at this academy, as he says he has "begun to draw the geometrical figures in a book," and he had also finished a map of South America, of which he was evidently proud. The boy was fond of drawing from his earliest childhood, and his "Sister Mary," afterwards Mrs. Atchison,[1] well remembered that, if ever their mother wanted to keep him quiet, she had only to supply him with a piece of paper and a pencil, and he would amuse himself for hours.

It is curious to note that, in spite of his instructresses being Quakers, the boy was already beginning to break away from the conventional "thou" and "thee," and uses the pronoun "you" once in his letter.

When the time arrived for his removal from a dame's establishment, the boy was transferred to a school for children of the Society of Friends at Hitchin, where he remained until nearly sixteen years of age, when, according to the custom of those days, a boy's scholastic education was considered to be complete. He received some rudimentary instruction in drawing at Hitchin from a master named Charles Parry,

[1] Mrs. Atchison, who died on 7th October 1906, survived all her brothers.

3rd mo 20th 1835

My dear Father

I hope thou and Brothers,
are quite well. when thou writes to
Mother give my very dear love, to her,
and when thou writes to Sister Mary
give my love to her also I shall be very
glad to hear from you I should be very
very much obliged to thee not to forget
to send me my Skipping Rope and my
knife. Cousin Elizabeth Foster came to see
me, and brought me a bag of Oranges
which were very nice indeed. I should
be very much obliged to thee to send me a

little writing paper. I have began to draw the Geometrical figures in a book, I have finished Reductions and am in Bills of Parcels I have finished the Map of South America, which I think looks very nice. If thou should go to Stannal will thou give my love to Robert, I received the bride cake yesterday, and am much obliged to thee ~Mother~ for sending it for me. Give my love to brothers, and Betsy, and accept it

thyself from, affectionate son
Myles Birket Foster

F.S. and P.Bar desire their remembran,

AT THE SPRING

SHELLING PEAS

THE BIRD'S NEST

GLEANERS

STEPPING-STONES

(An unfinished painting)

ARUNDEL PARK

(Unfinished)

PRIMROSES

SKETCH FOR "THE MILKMAID"

a man of some ability, for in 1843 a painting by him was exhibited in the Suffolk Street Galleries.

About this period Mr. Foster, senior, changed his residence to Stranraer Place, Maida Vale, and his son Birket continued to live under the family roof. "The Christmas Holly Cart," drawn for the *Illustrated London News* in 1848, was an actual scene from a window of a front room in the house, which was set apart as a studio for him.

Two years later, Birket Foster was married at Earsdon in Northumberland, on 13th August 1850, to his cousin, Ann Spence, a twin and tenth daughter of Robert Spence of North Shields, whose wife was a daughter of Robert Foster of Hebblethwaite Hall.

Mr. Foster, senior, removed to 12 Carlton Hill, St. John's Wood, and the newly-married couple took up their residence close by, at Marsden Villa in Clifton Road, now called Clifton Hill. The two houses stood back to back, with their gardens abutting, and a gateway was made in the wall to allow of easy communication between the two families. Subsequently Birket Foster removed to 12 Carlton Hill East. It was during his residence at these two abodes that his children, three sons and two daughters, were born, and while at the latter

that he had the great misfortune to lose his first
wife.   She died at Littlehampton on 4th July 1859.

It was also whilst Birket Foster was living in
Carlton Hill East that his father died on 21st
January 1861 at the good old age of seventy-six.
Owing to their names being the same, and their
addresses being very similar, the death of the father
was mistaken for that of the son, and in *The
Athenæum* of 2nd February of that year was the
following notice :—" Mr. Birket Foster, an artist
whose delicate pencil has been the delight of
Christmas homes for many years, died at his house
in St. John's Wood last week." We are glad to
add, however, that the mistake was duly rectified
in the next week's issue.   His eldest son Myles well

remembers the
look of surprise
on the faces of
two   worthy
ladies, who had
called to condole
with the children
at their sad loss,
when his father
himself opened
the door to them.

AT LANDELLS'

CHAPTER II

AT LANDELLS'

QUITTING school at an early age, young Birket Foster was at first placed in his father's business; but owing to an accident, he did not remain long in that position. In a speech made by the late Mr. John Foster a few years ago at an annual meeting of the shareholders, he stated: "It may be interesting to you to know that my brother, the celebrated water-colour artist, served for ten months in this business, but he cut his thigh in drawing a cork, and he found subsequently that his talent lay in another direction of drawing."

As the youth showed a decided tendency towards art, his father consulted a Mr. Stone, a die-engraver, with whom he had a slight acquaintance, and it was arranged that the son should be apprenticed to him. Before, however, the articles of apprenticeship could be signed, Mr. Stone unfortunately committed suicide. In his dilemma the father next sought the assistance of his fellow-townsman, Ebenezer Landells, who at that time had established his reputation as a wood-engraver. He offered to take the boy into his business to see whether the work would suit him. The offer was accepted, and the day on which Birket Foster entered Landells' office may be said to be the commencement of that artistic career in which he was afterwards to become so famous.

Ebenezer Landells was born at Newcastle-on-Tyne in 1808, and was apprenticed by his father to Thomas Bewick, with whom he became a favourite pupil. On the death of his master Landells came to London, and after some time set up in business on his own account as a wood-engraver. Landells was a fine tall man of genial disposition and had a generous heart. He possessed considerable enterprise, and started several illustrated newspapers, but, like most pioneers, he never made a fortune.

Amongst his friends he was known as "Daddy" Landells, owing to the length of his legs, whilst amongst his employés he went by the sobriquet of "Tooch-it-oop," from his strong Northumbrian accent. Landells at first set young Birket Foster to work at trying his hand in cutting wood-blocks, but he did not make much progress in this direction, and Landells, soon discovering that the boy's ability lay in drawing, employed him henceforward as a draughtsman, and from that time onwards many hundreds of wood-blocks were destined to be drawn upon by his pencil. He, however, whilst with Landells, continued to do some wood-engraving, and many of his own small drawings were cut by himself.

At Landells' office, which at that time was at 76 Fleet Street, Birket Foster first met amongst his fellow-workers John Greenaway, the father of Kate Greenaway, and Edmund Evans, who afterwards became the well-known colour-printer. Between Birket Foster and the latter a close intimacy sprang up, which existed without interruption during the remainder of their lives. Evans was a year younger than Birket Foster, and had been apprenticed to Landells some little time before the latter's arrival. He lived in early youth on the south side of the Thames between Bermondsey and Rotherhithe. He

had a vivid recollection of a picturesque old farmyard
on the south side of the Old Kent Road with grey
barns and a straw-yard with cows and chickens;
and near to it was the "Green Man" toll-gate,

EDMUND EVANS AND JOHN GREENAWAY.

.through which in the evenings he saw four-horsed
coaches pass on their outward journey bearing the
mails, and with "Tonbridge Wells," "Dover," and
"Paris" on their panels. Evans left school before
he was fourteen years of age, and was placed in
Samuel Bentley's printing office, Bangor House,
Shoe Lane, with the intention of becoming a
compositor, this being considered a suitable
occupation for him as he was a thin and delicate
boy—so thin, that amongst his relatives "As thin

as Edmund " was a common expression. The first
step towards becoming a compositor was to be a
reader's boy, but as he had a nervous impediment in
his speech it was soon found that he was of no use
for the post, and he was accordingly transferred to
the warehouse department, where he became little
more than an errand-boy. The firm had a good
reputation for printing from wood-engravings, and
it was here that the boy first saw a wood-block,
and he was greatly interested in it. He made
an attempt to copy one which was being printed
for a book for John Van Voorst of Paternoster
Row. It was a mule engraved by Vasey for
Yarrell's *Natural History*; he scratched this
animal on a thick piece of slate, and then tried to
take impressions from it during the dinner-hour
when the presses were unoccupied, the result being
that he was summoned before one of the heads of
the firm for meddling with the printing press.
Fortunately his master did not look upon the crime
in a very severe light, but discovered that there was
latent talent in the small boy. A letter of introduction to Ebenezer Landells was given to young
Evans, and he was at once apprenticed to him as
a wood-engraver.

Soon after Birket Foster's arrival Landells moved

his establishment to Bidborough Street, and having plenty of work in hand his staff was frequently kept till the early hours of the morning, executing wood-blocks for the illustrated newspapers. The

long hours told upon the delicate young Evans, and he was often incapacitated for engraving the next day. Landells, however, was a good-hearted man, and on these occasions sent Evans with Birket Foster on his sketching expeditions near and around London. The two young men had many tastes in common, and these rambles together helped

EDMUND EVANS.   considerably to cement their friendship. They went to Blackwall by the railway when the carriages were drawn by ropes and stationary engines. From Blackwall they visited the Isle of Dogs in search of picturesque scenery, which was then to be found there. There were pleasant meadows with cattle grazing, surrounded with dykes. On one occasion Evans remembered that they wasted the whole day rambling about, and all sketching was forgotten. As Landells required the next morning to see the result of the

day's work, Birket Foster when he returned home
made some sketches from E. W. Cooke's *Etchings
of Shipping and Craft*. When Landells saw them
he exclaimed, "Capital, Foster! There is nothing
like going to nature." Evans added this was the
only incident of the kind, for Birket Foster was a
most conscientious worker, and loved his drawing
too well to shirk it.

On other occasions they took the train to
Croydon, which was then a terminus, and walked
to Waddon, Beddington Park, Saunderstead, and
other surrounding villages in search of the picturesque. They also journeyed to Rochester, where
they found much to engage their attention, and on
their visiting the old church at Swanscombe on
a very wet day the clayey soil was so sticky that
it pulled the soles off their boots, and they had to
tie them on with string.

Once they extended their travels by going in
an excursion train as far as Dover. The third-
class carriages in those early days of railways
were simply open trucks with seats, having no
protection against the weather. It happened to
be a rainy day, and the water which collected on
the floor of the carriage from the dripping of the
umbrellas made the journey most uncomfortable,

Dover 3rd Class Excursion Trip

and the dust and grime from the engine which they experienced in passing through the tunnels did not add to their comfort.

Whilst they were at Bidborough Street the two youths frequently took their mid-day meals in the fields close to St. Pancras Church; it was then quite open country all the way to Hampstead and Highgate.

Owing to increase of work and the desirability of being close to the newspaper offices, Landells removed his establishment to St. Bride's Court, Fleet Street. The engraving-room here overlooked the churchyard of St. Bride's Church, where the staff witnessed some gruesome sights. An old grave-digger used to explore the small burying-

ground with a long iron, with a cross piece for a
handle at the top, which they nicknamed the
cheese - taster.   He progged this iron in the
ground until he found a sufficiently clear space to
dig a grave, and then erected a screen to hide from
public view the
large amount of
skulls and bones
which he dug up.

The life of em-
ployés and ap-
prentices sixty
years ago was very
primitive com-
pared with the
ordinary living of
the present time,
which would have
been considered
luxurious in those
days. Notwithstanding this, the young men enjoyed themselves with their frugal repasts. Evans
was appointed cook, and in that capacity had
frequently not only to buy a joint of meat but to
peel potatoes, which were taken to a neighbouring
bakehouse to be cooked. Evans was also some-

4

times deputed to cook a chop or steak for Landells' lunch.   On one occasion in turning the steak on the gridiron it fell into the ash-pan; in an instant it was under a tap, washed with cold water, and then back on the gridiron again.   Landells declared it was the best-cooked steak he had ever tasted.

Whilst they were at St. Bride's Birket Foster and Evans frequently went to the river-side, and into the yards of the wharfingers, which were entered from the bottom of Salisbury Court and Bouverie Street.   Here they used to watch the barges with brown-coloured sails on their way to and from Hungerford Market, and make sketches of these as well as the picturesque windlasses and tackle on the wharves.

From St. Bride's Court Landells again moved his establishment, in 1846, to Holford Square, Pentonville.   About this time Birket Foster had completed his engagement with Landells, and commenced to take commissions for drawings for book and newspaper illustrations on his own account, whilst Evans, to his great regret, had to serve the last year of his apprenticeship without his boon companion.   Early in the summer of that year, however, he had a most delightful holiday with Birket

Foster and his elder brother Dodshon. These three young men took a steamboat from a wharf near the Tower, and made a trip by sea to Berwick-on-Tweed. Here they stayed for some little time; Birket Foster and Edmund Evans enjoyed themselves by making sketching tours in the vicinity, whilst Dodshon Foster devoted himself to collecting sea birds' eggs, of which he found a great quantity on the rocks of the neighbouring islands, including those of the guillemot, puffin, eider-duck, and many other varieties. They hired a boat and visited in turn Holy Island, where they were delighted with the old grey ruins of the Priory Church and Monastery, and the Farne Islands. Here they went over Longstone Lighthouse, then kept by old Darling, and saw the rooms in which Grace Darling had lived—she had died of consumption a few years previously. They extended their visits to Bamborough Castle, and farther south as far as the river Coquet to see the hermitage of Sir Bertram and the remains of old Warkworth Castle, both charmingly situated above the river. The two artists were greatly impressed with the beauty of the Northumbrian scenery, and especially with some wonderful sunsets which occurred during their stay. Our travellers next took a steamboat

to Leith and explored Edinburgh; thence they
went to Stirling, Loch Katrine, and the Trossachs.
On their way back to London they visited Birket
Foster's native town, North Shields, where they
stayed with his uncle, Mr. Robert Spence, a member
of the Society of Friends, who warmly entertained
the young men. This was the first visit Birket
Foster had made to the North since his father had
brought him to London sixteen years previously,
and the first occasion on which he had crossed the
Border. Scotland had a peculiar attraction for
him, and he visited the country north of the
Tweed again and again, as is evinced by the
numerous drawings of Scottish scenery by his
hand which are in existence.

Shortly after this first tour Birket Foster paid
his second visit to Scotland with his brother
Dodshon, the former to make sketches, and the
latter to collect birds' eggs as on the former
occasion. This time they extended their travels
as far as the Shetland Isles. On their way back to
the mainland they got into conversation with the
captain of the steamboat, and sat down on a
large case marked "Eggs with care," listening to
his yarns. Amongst other tales he told them that
a great benefactor to the islands had recently died

THE MILKMAID

PLAYMATES

TYNEMOUTH FROM CULLERCOATS

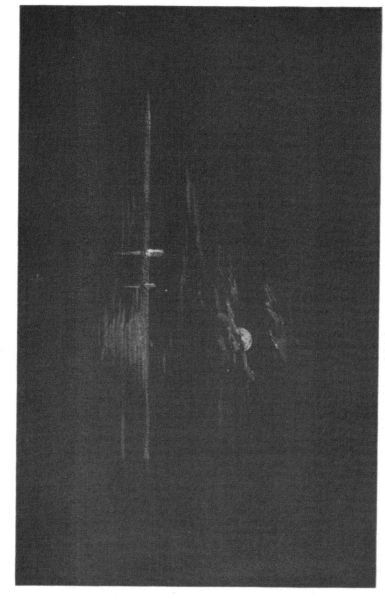

A MOONLIGHT EFFECT

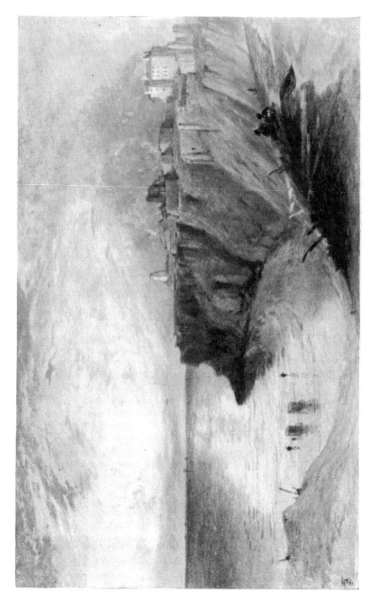

TYNEMOUTH

GOING HOME

THE CHRISTMAS HOLLY CART

SHELLING PEAS

(An unfinished painting)

there, and he was bringing the body back to Scotland for burial in the family vault. On their enquiring where it was, he explained in a hoarse whisper, "You are sitting on it noo!" and went on to explain that owing to the prejudice of the sailors against having dead bodies on board the ship, he was obliged to conceal it from their knowledge.

"PUNCH" AND "THE ILLUSTRATED LONDON NEWS"

CHAPTER III

"PUNCH" AND "THE ILLUSTRATED LONDON NEWS"

ALTHOUGH Ebenezer Landells started several illustrated newspapers, which had but an ephemeral existence, he was the original projector of a weekly paper, the name of which is still a household word at the present time.   Landells was attracted by the French comic paper *Le Charivari*, and he conceived the idea of an English publication on similar lines. He communicated his scheme to a printer named

J. Last. These two men called in the aid of some literary men, and eventually on the 17th July 1841 the first number of *Punch* appeared. It was a joint undertaking, Landells having one share, Henry Mayhew, Mark Lemon, and Stirling Coyne a second share, and J. Last a third share. The name *Punch* is supposed to have originated from the fact of Mark Lemon being connected with it as its first editor, and Birket Foster remembered that when Landells announced the title to his apprentices they considered it to be a very silly one, and it was little thought that it would become such an important publication.

Landells retained his interest in *Punch* for about two years only, when Messrs. Bradbury and Evans acquired his share, and eventually became sole proprietors. Most of the early wood-cuts were engraved in Landells' office, and Birket Foster, although but still a youth, was employed to draw and cut numerous initial letters and some small illustrations. The following is a list of the initial letters which were executed by him :—

VOLUME I

Page 85, letter O. A life-guardsman jumping through a wreath.
„ 142 „ O. Wreath of flowers surrounding a hay cart, and sunset.

The letter G, p. 262, and a lady praying, p. 262, both copies of drawings by Gavarni, were also drawn and cut by Birket Foster. Also many other small engravings were produced in silhouette by him; they were technically called "blackies."

Most, if not all, the initial letters, were at first executed for a projected journal called *Cosmorama*, which Landells intended to publish, but he abandoned it when *Punch* was issued. The initial letter T, with shipping, of the introduction in the first number of the latter was drawn by H. G. Hine and cut by Birket Foster for the *Cosmorama*.

For these little drawings the magnificent remuneration of eighteenpence apiece was paid. On one
occasion Birket Foster was entrusted with a full
page cartoon, which appeared on the 11th December
1841, "Punch's Pencillings, No. xxii, Jack cutting
his Name on a Beam."   It represented Lord John
Russell, and was a parody on an etching by George
Cruikshank of Jack Sheppard.

During this period many literary men and
artists connected with *Punch*, including Mark
Lemon, Douglas Jerrold, Henry and Horace
Mayhew, G. à Beckett, John Gilbert, Alfred
Forrester (A. Crowquill), H. K. Brown (Phiz),
and William Harvey, frequently called at Landells'
establishment and all had a cheery word to say to
his employés ; but Thackeray, who drew on wood-
blocks as well as wrote for *Punch*, used to march

past them with his long strides without uttering a word.

After Landells had lost his interest in *Punch*, he brought out *Mephistopheles* and other comic papers as rivals to it, but none of them were successful enterprises, and were soon discontinued. Landells also started *The Illuminated Magazine*, which was edited by Douglas Jerrold. They were intimate friends, and on one occasion Jerrold, whilst staying at Greenwich, sent the following invitation to Landells :

Come where the gas lights quiver
Down by the muddy river ;
Bring Mrs. L. and the kids as well,
And lots of tin we'll disciver.

"Lots of tin" evidently referred to the projected publication.

About this period *The Illustrated London News* was started by Herbert Ingram, and the first number appeared on 14th May 1842. Landells was engaged to produce many of the illustrations, and Birket Foster was employed by him in making drawings for them. This he continued to do for many years after he left Landells' establishment. He drew illustrations of the popular events of the day, such as the Oxford and Cambridge boat race, but to these he rarely added his name or initials ;

whilst on the rural scenes, which he executed with such poetic feeling, the name B. Foster is generally to be found. The first illustration on which his name occurs is a small one; it appeared in July 1846, and was a view of the ruins of Tynemouth Priory, close to his native town, North Shields. The name of Foster may be discerned on one of the gravestones.

Two years later, in March 1848, he drew ".A Rush for the Daily Newspapers," representing *The London Telegraph* Office, a picturesque old house, two doors from St. Dunstan's Church on the north side of Fleet Street, which had escaped the Fire of London, but has long since been pulled down. A mob of news-vendors are crowding at the entrance to the office to get their supplies, containing the latest news of the Revolution in Paris. This paper was published every day at twelve o'clock, "with all the news received by the post of the same morning, and the amazing quick intelligence received by Electric Telegraph, which conquers Time and Space. The Electric Telegraph, with communications completed to the most important districts will revolutionise all our social relations, and with it the Daily Press of London." So stated the Prospectus of *The London Telegraph*, priced threepence. A very different state of affairs from those of the present day, when every one reads the latest news at his breakfast table: truly the Daily Press of London has been revolutionised by telegraphy since that date.

In June of the same year Birket Foster was sent to Portsmouth to make sketches of the opening of the new steam basin by H.M. Queen Victoria. Two wood-cuts appeared from his drawings, "The Mayor of Portsmouth presenting an Address to the Queen," and "*The Fairy* entering the New Basin." A reproduction of his original sketch for the former is between pp. 44–45.

The Queen came in *The Fairy* from Osborne to attend this ceremony, and an additional *éclat* was given to the event, as this was the first occasion on which Her Majesty "had presented herself to her loyal subjects in so public a manner since the memorable 10th April (the Chartist Meeting), when the security of the Throne received so remarkable and decided a guarantee from the conduct of the nation at large." A little incident nearly gave rise to a very awkward consequence. Whilst the Queen was standing on the platform, and the ceremony which she had come to witness was proceeding, a police inspector was instructed to go and tell the band to play " Rule Britannia." This official in the violence of his zeal rushed forward with such headlong haste to give the necessary order that he very nearly knocked Her Majesty down.

In 1849 Birket Foster, who had left Landells three years previously, and was working on his own account, was commissioned by the proprietors of the *Illustrated London News* to visit the different watering-places in England, and to make a series of drawings of their chief features, which were subsequently reproduced in their journal. The first to appear was a view of Worthing in August of that year, and it was followed by Hastings in the next month, and Bridlington Quay in October.   Birket Foster was accompanied by his friend Edmund Evans on these tours, and most, if not all, of the wood-blocks were engraved by him.   These commissions gave them many very delightful journeys, and although their remuneration did not include the travelling expenses, both these young men considered that they were amply repaid in consequence of the great enjoyment they obtained from these visits to the sea-coast.   In 1850 the two friends went to Folkestone and Dover, likewise to Budleigh Salterton, illustrations of these places appearing in July and August. They also went to Birket Foster's native town, and a view of Tynemouth Harbour from the Priory was the result. On their way back to London they stayed at Doncaster to witness the races, and two drawings by Foster, "The Road to the Course" and "The Race Course," were reproduced in September. For the latter drawing they selected a position about midway down the course to see the horses sweep round the bend. In one of the races, a horse came too close to the rails and fell; the jockey was thrown and the horse nearly rolled over him. The accident caused considerable commotion, and some horsemen quickly rode up to ascertain what injuries had been sustained. Much to our artists' disgust the first inquiry was, "Is she hurt?" referring to the horse, no notice being taken of the jockey. In the next year, 1851, no less than six illustrations of different sea-side resorts appeared; two from the south coast, Sidmouth and Star Cross; three from Kent—Margate, Broadstairs and Sandgate; and another view of Tynemouth.

In 1852 Eastbourne was reproduced, and in the same year the first of the inland spas, Matlock-Bath, appeared. It was followed by Buxton in

6

1854, and Harrogate in 1856. In this, the last, year of the appearance of these views, Birket Foster and Evans visited the Lancashire coast, and illustrations of Blackpool, Lytham, and Southport were the result of their genial labours. All these holiday resorts in the middle of the nineteenth century were primitive places, as may be seen from the illustrations, and very different from the large towns which most of them have now become.

The most characteristic works of Birket Foster in the *Illustrated London News* were the charming engravings which appeared in the musical supplements and the Christmas numbers. The first of the former was issued in June 1848, entitled "Peace at Home." The lines were written by G. Douglas Thompson, and the music by Edward J. Loder. For this Birket Foster drew a head-piece in three compartments, the centre representing a harvest scene, and on either side cottagers seated by a fire, and labourers lading a ship in a dock. In the following year there were four musical supplements, entitled "Spring," "Summer," "Autumn," and "Winter." The poetry for these was written by Charles Mackay, and Birket Foster executed head-pieces for all of them. "Spring—the Invitation to the Fields," represented by children gathering wild flowers in a wood beside a road; "Summer Shades," by cattle in a stream and a boy asleep on a bank; "An Autumnal Lyric," illustrated by men working in the harvest-field; and "Winter," by a snow scene. There was also another supplement in the month of May of this year, entitled "May Lyrics," with verses by C. Mackay, and illustrated by five engravings after drawings by Birket Foster; and in May 1850 "A Song of Spring," by Desmond Ryan, with a heading of some milkmaids talking to a seated ploughman by our artist. These were followed by "The Cuckoo" and "The Light of Love" in December 1851; and in the next month, January 1852, "The Mother's Lament" and "The Green Lanes of England"; in May "Wild Flowers"; and June of the same year, "The Dreams of Youth." For all these musical pieces Birket Foster supplied illustrations.

The Christmas numbers of the *Illustrated London News* were without rivals during the middle of last century, and the most popular illustrators of the time were commissioned to make drawings for them. John Gilbert, John Leach, Kenny Meadows, and others drew the jovial scenes of the festive season, whilst it was reserved to Birket Foster to supply those country and domestic scenes which appeal to the poetic feelings of the Yuletide. His first drawing for a Christmas number appeared in 1848. A reproduction of it faces this page. At this period of his life he was residing with his parents at Stranraer Place, Maida Vale, where one of the rooms was given up to him to serve as a studio. Looking out of the window one winter's morning his attention was attracted by their servant purchasing some holly from a cart drawn by a donkey. The subject pleased him, and he made a hasty sketch, which he afterwards drew upon a wood-block. His sister admiring the rough sketch, Birket Foster worked upon it with water-colours, and presented it to her at Christmas. This is probably one of his earliest water-colour paintings. The editor of the *Illustrated London News*, by way of a joke, inserted beneath the engraving, "The Christmas Holly Cart drawn by B. Foster," and the artist had to accept a bushel of good-natured chaff from his friends, respecting this title for many a day.

A similar scene under a different garb, entitled " Spring Time in London," appeared in April 1850. There are the same donkey and cart, but with flowers " all a-blowing and a-growing," which a man is exchanging for old clothes with his customers.

MYLES BIRKET FOSTER, SENIOR.

BIRKET FOSTER WHEN A YOUNG MAN.
From a Daguerreotype portrait.

THE MAYOR OF PORTSMOUTH PRESENTING THE ADDRESS TO THE QUEEN.

From an original sketch for the "Illustrated London News," 3rd June, 1848.

THE VILLAGE WAITS.
From an original sketch for the "Illustrated London News," Christmas, 1853.

THE MISTLETOE SELLER.

Original sketch for the engraving in the "Illustrated London News." *Christmas,* 1854.

CHRISTMAS EVE. THE COTTAGER'S RETURN FROM MARKET.
Original sketch for the engraving in the "Illustrated London News." Christmas, 1855.

MAY.

From an original sketch for the "Illustrated London Almanack," 1848.

NEWCASTLE-ON-TYNE.

From an original sketch.

On the following Christmas his contribution was the winter scene already mentioned—the musical and Christmas supplements being combined.

There were five engravings in the Christmas number for 1850, four representing town life—one the distribution of coals to the poor, and another "The Grocer's Shop at Christmas," and two, "Frozen-out Gardeners" and "Snow-Sweepers." These, however, were subjects hardly so suitable to his pencil as the fifth—a country road in winter with a coach, laden with boys going home for the holidays, overtaking a carrier's cart. In the following year he made a drawing for a full-page illustration, entitled "The Christmas Hearth," and a smaller one, "Gathering Mistletoe." On the next Christmas he gave a landscape entitled " A Winter Scene," and in the three following years appeared wood-engravings of "The Village Waits," "The Cottager's Return from Market," and "The Mistletoe Seller," of which reproductions of the original sketches are given.

In 1855 the first coloured engraving appeared in the *Illustrated London News,* and on the following Christmas Birket Foster supplied a drawing for a coloured plate, entitled " Winter." At Christmas 1857 a large double-page illustration was given,

entitled "The Happy Homes of England—Christmas Holidays."

> The stately Homes of England,—
> How beautiful they stand,
> Amidst their tall ancestral trees,
> O'er all the pleasant land.
> The deer across the greensward bound
> Through shade and sunshine gleam,
> And the swan glides past them with the sound
> Of some rejoicing stream.

The drawing was by Birket Foster, and the engraving printed in colours by Leighton Brothers.

"Christmas—the cottage door," appeared in
1859, and after this period Birket Foster gradually
ceased his connection with the *Illustrated London
News*. In addition to the musical supplements and
Christmas numbers, engravings after his drawings
are to be found dispersed throughout the journal.
For instance during the year 1851 "Hot Cross
Buns," "Maying," "Please to remember the Grotto,"
"Guy Fawkes Day—burning a Guy," all characteristic engravings, appeared. In 1853 there
was a large double-page panoramic view of Con-
stantinople from the Tower of Galata drawn by
Birket Foster from a sketch by Samuel Read, this
city at that time, just before the Crimean War,
was attracting much attention; and in 1856 the

illuminations in celebration of the Peace took place, and an illustration is given of Birket Foster's preliminary sketch for these at the Royal Exchange.

In 1845 *The Illustrated London Almanack* was brought out by the proprietors of the *Illustrated London News.* The first issue, besides having numerous wood-engravings, contains general information for the benefit of the public, and some of the paragraphs form curious reading at the present time. For instance, under New Railway Regulations it states that by an Act passed by Parliament during the late session, known as Mr. Gladstone's Railway Bill, the following additional provision is made for the accommodation of the public by railway conveyance : — "The carriages in which passengers shall be conveyed by such trains shall be provided with seats, and shall be protected from the weather in a manner satisfactory to the Lords of the Committee of Privy Council for Trade and Plantations." Consequently our artist had no longer to suffer uncomfortable journeys, such as on the occasion of his trip to Dover with his friend Edmund Evans three years previously, when umbrellas afforded them the only protection from the rain.

Particulars setting forth the amount to be paid

annually for the Window Tax are also given, and
we learn in that year there were only nine theatres
in London.

In the *Almanack* for the year 1848 there were
twenty-four wood-engravings of country scenes,
two for each month, after drawings by Birket
Foster, accompanied by descriptions by Thomas
Miller. They are all charming illustrations of
rural occupations carried on during the various
months, and are by far the best in the *Almanack*;
but our artist, being still a youth at this time, it
was not deemed necessary to mention his name,
although that of Kenny Meadows, who drew
some vulgar heads representing the months, is
given in the index of contents.

These drawings were followed in the next year
by another set of country scenes, two for every
month, which are equally charming, and on this
occasion the name of B. Foster appears as the
artist.

For the *Almanack* for the year 1853 Birket Foster
designed the title page, on which the four seasons
are represented by small pictures of " Children
gathering Wild-flowers," "Haymaking," "Harvest,"
and "An Old Man carrying Faggots." He also
made a drawing for each month, but instead of

rural scenes he gave the recreations enjoyed by the residents of London at various periods during the year. Fifty-three years ago life was much more simple, and the ordinary Londoner was content with much quieter enjoyments, than at the present day, as shown by these illustrations, such as "Skating on the Ice in the Parks"; "An Evening Party"; "A Trip to Gravesend"; "A Visit to the Zoological Gardens"; "Acting Charades"; and "A Christmas Tree."

BOOK ILLUSTRATIONS

THE LOLLARD'S TOWER, LAMBETH PALACE.
From a pencil and wash sketch.

PEACE ILLUMINATIONS.

From an original sketch for the "Illustrated London News," 1856.

A LANDSCAPE.

A pencil and wash Drawing.

CHRISTMAS TIME.   DISTRIBUTING GIFTS TO THE POOR.
From a pencil and wash sketch.

CHAPTER IV

BOOK ILLUSTRATIONS

WHILST Birket Foster was at Landells' office he assisted in making drawings for wood-engravings for books as well as for illustrated newspapers. The first book with which he was connected was *Ireland : Its Scenery, Character, etc.,* by Mr. and Mrs. S. Carter Hall, published in 1841 by Messrs. How and Parsons ; it is a curious coincidence that this should have been the only part of the British Isles Birket Foster never visited. The engravings for *Richmond and other Poems,* by C. Ellis, brother of Sir J.

Whittaker Ellis, Bart., bear Landells' signature as engraver, and were cut from Birket Foster's drawings, although his name is not recorded. Other pictorial publications were similarly illustrated by him at this period.

At Landells' recommendation Birket Foster used to copy line engravings in pen and ink, so as

to learn how to represent colour by various strengths of lines.[1] Jacob Bell, the founder of the Pharmaceutical Society and donor of the fine collection of

[1] The illustration of Quilp and his wife, reproduced in pen and ink by Birket Foster from an engraving after Hablot K. Browne's drawing in the first edition of *Master Humphrey's Clock* in 1840, shows the precision with which he could make these copies, and, if it were not for the B. F. in the corner, it might easily be mistaken for the original engraving.

paintings to the National Gallery, being a friend
of Birket Foster's father, lent the youth some of
the engravings after Landseer's paintings for the
purpose of making copies, and Mrs. Black, the
daughter of the late Mrs. Atchison, still possesses
a pen-and-ink drawing made from the engraving of
The Highland Breakfast.

Shortly before his apprenticeship expired with
Landells, an accident happened, which threatened
to put an end to his short career. Whilst on a
holiday tour in the Highlands with his brother
Dodshon, they were being driven in a carriage near
Aberfeldy when it overturned. Birket Foster's right
arm was broken in two places, and he received some
injury in his back. The use of the injured arm was
fortunately restored in a comparatively short space
of time, although it was badly set by a local surgeon,
and he refused to allow it to be re-set by a
specialist on his return to London. But for seven
months he was confined to his bed by the other
affliction. Grievous as the cessation from work
must have been, it still afforded him an opportunity
for mental study, and for learning to draw with his
left hand. With reference to this enforced idleness,
his own opinion was that a season of entire rest
from practice of his own defects in art is the most

beneficial time for an artist. Upon his recovery he went back to Landells for a short time to complete the term he had agreed to serve him. He finally left, not without feelings of regret, in 1846. Birket Foster had always in after life a good word to say for his generous and kind-hearted master.

When our artist was free to work on his own account he was not long in obtaining many commissions. He was, at first, greatly assisted by Henry Vizetelly, a well-known engraver and printer, and through his introduction Birket Foster made the drawings for *The Boys' Country Book*, written by Thomas Miller, and published in 1847, by Chapman and Hall, in four parts. From the small illustrations in these books it may be seen that Foster was then greatly under the influence of Bewick, whose engravings he was accustomed to copy in his juvenile days.

His first great success was the illustrations to *Evangeline* by Longfellow, published by David Bogue in 1850. In reviewing this work *The Athenæum* stated, " A more lovely book than this has rarely been given to the public ; Mr. Foster's designs in particular have a picturesque grace and elegance, which recall the pleasure we experienced on our first examination of Mr. Roger's *Italy* when it came before us illustrated by persons of no less refinement and invention than Stothard and Turner. Any one disposed to carp at our praise as overstrained is invited to consider the 'Boat on the Mississippi,' which, to our thinking, is a jewel of the first water." This book was followed in the next year by *Voices of the Night and other Poems* by Longfellow, and *Christmas with the Poets*, with fifty illustrations by Birket Foster, engraved by Vizetelly and printed in tints of grey, brown, and brownish pink, with a gold line border; in the two following years Bogue published Longfellow's *Poetical Works*, illustrated by upwards of one hundred engravings on wood from drawings by Birket Foster, Jane L. Benham (afterwards Mrs. Benham Hay), and others; and *Hyperion*, for which Foster paid his first visit to the Rhine accompanied by Henry Vizetelly, who engraved the illustrations. Birket Foster evidently laid great store on these early drawings made on the Continent, for they were still in his possession at the time of his death. They were afterwards sold at Christie's.

About the same time as Foster was apprenticed to Landells, Joseph Cundall came up from Norwich and entered the establishment of Messrs. Tilt and

8

Bogue; whilst there he first made Foster's acquaintance.

He was one of the pioneers of the improvement in illustrated books for children, which at the early part of the nineteenth century were crudely printed and coarsely illustrated. The first book he brought out on his own account, when a young man of twenty-three years of age, and still employed by Tilt and Bogue, was *Robin Hood and his Merry Men*, with illustrations by John Gilbert; these were coloured by hand. Afterwards, when he entered business on his own account at 12 Old Bond Street—where there still exists a reminiscence of his artistic taste in two brackets on the exterior, executed by John Bell the sculptor—he published, in conjunction with Sir Henry Cole, who wrote under the *nom de plume* of Felix Summerly, "The Home Treasury," a series of books for children. These little volumes were well printed in fine old-faced type by Charles Whittingham of the Chiswick Press, and were illustrated by the best artists of the day, amongst them being J. C. Horsley, T. Webster, C. W. Cope, Richard Redgrave, and John Absolon. In *Fraser's Magazine* for April 1846 Thackeray writes: "As there is no person of the late Mr. Fielding's powers of writing in this magazine, let me be permitted humbly to move a vote of thanks to the meritorious Mr. Cundall. The mere sight of the little books published by Mr. Cundall, of which some thirty now lie upon my table, is as good as a nosegay."

Joseph Cundall next turned his attention to illustrating volumes of poems, which were much in demand as Christmas gift-books for many years. The first of these appeared in 1849, entitled *Songs, Madrigals and Sonnets: A gathering of some of the most Pleasant Flowers of Old English Poetry*. It bears the name of Longman and Co. as publishers, and contains a preface written by J. C. from Camden Cottages. Each page is surrounded by a coloured border ornamented with arabesques in double lines of different colours, many of them enclosing vignettes. The whole is designed in an old Italian style to suit the supposed origin of the sonnet or madrigal, and in a note it is stated that the ornamental borders in this book have been printed by means of wood-blocks.

The next books published by Joseph Cundall were *Poetical Works of Oliver Goldsmith* (1851) and Gray's *Elegy written in a Country Churchyard* (1854): both these volumes were illustrated by Birket Foster. In the former the illustrations were elaborately printed in colours. Birket Foster first made his drawings direct on the wood in the usual manner, and after Evans had engraved the design he pulled a proof of the block on drawing-paper for Birket Foster's use ; the latter then coloured it, and Evans made the various blocks required for the different colours. The same colours were employed in the printing, as the artist had used in making the coloured drawings in order to obtain a faithful reproduction. During the following ten years J. Cundall brought out many other gift-books adorned with engravings after drawings by Birket Foster and other artists. Although they were published for him by such firms as David Bogue, Bell and Daldy, and Sampson Low and Co., still his monogram of J. C. may be found at the back of the title pages of many of them. The most important of these works, with illustrations by Birket Foster, were *Rhymes and Roundelays in Praise of a Country Life* (1856) ; *Mia and Charlie*, by Harriet Myrtle (1856), published by Bogue ; *Sabbath Bells chimed by the Poets*, with illustrations in colour (1856), and Burns' *Songs and Poems* (1857), published by Bell and Daldy ; *The Pleasures of Hope*, by Thomas Campbell (1856) ; *The Farmer's Boy*, by Robert Bloomfield (1857) ; *The Rime of the Ancient Mariner* (1857); *The*

Poetical Works of Edgar Allen Poe (1858); *Pastoral Poems*, by Wordsworth (1859); *Favourite English Poems* (1859); *The Hamlet*, an ode written in Whichwood Forest, by Thomas Warton (1859); *Poetical Works of Thomas Gray* (1859); and *The Merchant of Venice* (1860)—all published by Sampson Low and Co. ; and *A Book of Favourite Modern Ballads* (1860), by Kent and Co. After Foster had relinquished drawing for wood-engraving Cundall produced *Summer Scenes*, a series of photographs from some of Birket Foster's choicest water-colours; it was published by Bell and Daldy in 1867.

When Edmund Evans' term of seven years with Landells expired in May 1847 he commenced business as a wood-engraver, at first at his private residence, and afterwards at Wine Office Court, next to the "Old Cheshire Cheese." At the latter place he started a hand-printing press, but the early hours of his workmen and the noise of the press annoyed a quiet lawyer who had rooms beneath. He consequently removed to 4 Racquet Court, Fleet Street, where "The Racquet Press," so well known for its colour-printing, existed until the house was pulled down a few years ago and the business removed to Southwark.

The first wood-block which Evans engraved on his own account was a vignette for a book written by a Mr. Fisk—" A View of Bethany," drawn by Birket Foster—and the first commission received from the proprietors of *The Illustrated London News* was a view of Rydal Mount, where the poet laureate Wordsworth lived, and two other small engravings. To his regret, however, Nathaniel Cooke, who was partner with Herbert Ingram, told Evans that he was willing to give him more work, but his engraving was not quite good enough —the fact being that he engraved the blocks in a too fine manner, fitted only for books and not bold enough for newspaper work. Fortunately, at the time he had a commission in hand to cut the block for " The Christmas Holly Cart," drawn by Birket Foster, as already mentioned. This he executed in a much broader manner, and it was quite a success; afterwards nearly all of the wood blocks drawn by Birket Foster for *The Illustrated London News* were engraved by Evans.

Ingram, Cooke and Co. carried on a publishing business, called the " Universal Library," in the Strand, not far from the offices of their journal, of which Ebenezer Ward, afterwards a partner in the firm of Ward and Lock, was manager. Evans stated that he received much kindness from Nathaniel Cooke, and through him was given plenty of work in engraving for book illustrations. Amongst the first were the illustrations to Madame Ida Pfeiffer's *Travels in the Holy Land, Egypt, and Italy* (1851), by Birket Foster. These he must have copied from other drawings, as there is nothing characteristic of his own style in them, and he never went as far as Palestine or Egypt. The engravings were printed in a grey and warm tint. This was followed by *Fern Leaves from Fanny's Portfolio* (1853), and *Little Ferns for Fanny's Little Friends* (1854), both written by Miss G. P. Willis under the pseudonym of "Fanny Fern," with illustrations by Foster printed with tints. The engravings for *The Poetical Works of Oliver Goldsmith*, by Birket Foster, already mentioned, were also printed in tints by Evans.

Soon afterwards Edmund Evans originated the idea of printing coloured illustrations on book covers. The first—"Letters Left at a Pastry Cook's," for Ingram, Cooke and Co.—was simply a letter with several re-directions, some in red letters, some in black, and the background consisting of a dark blue printed over red. The second was more pictorial in character, "The Log of the Water

Lily," drawn by Birket Foster, and effectively printed in a dark grey blue mingled with strong warm tints. These two were printed on white paper, and several similar book covers followed. The trade, however, required a toned paper so that the covers should not soil too readily, and yellow enamelled paper was used, the books thus bound becoming popularly known as " Yellow Backs." Messrs. Routledge and Co., and other firms, brought out a large number of books with these covers, and the most popular artists of the day were engaged to execute the designs, including Birket Foster, John Gilbert, H. K. Browne (Phiz), George Cruikshank, Charles Keene, and a host of others. The drawing was first cut on a wood-block in the ordinary manner, then two "transfers" from the block, *i.e.* impressions whilst wet laid down on plain blocks, then passed through a press so that the wet impressions were "set off" on the plain blocks. These were then cut, one being used for the red and the other for the blue printing. The former was engraved in gradations so as to obtain light tints for faces and hands, whilst the latter was cut so as to get the best result of texture patterns or sky, and by crossing the blue over the red effects of light and shade were obtained. In

some cases green ink was used instead of blue.
These covers attracted the public taste so much
at that time that publishers frequently gave orders
for an illustrated cover for a remnant they had in
stock, and not only were they able to sell off the
remnant by this means, but often a reprint was
demanded. Three specimens of these covers, designed by Birket Foster, are given facing page 64.

The publishers of the present volume, Messrs.
A. and C. Black, employed Birket Foster to draw
the illustrations for four of Sir Walter Scott's
works, *The Lay of the Last Minstrel* (1853); *The
Lady of the Lake* (1854); *Marmion* (1855); and
The Lord of the Isles (1857). For these works
Foster went specially to Scot-
land to make his drawings, and
was accompanied on each occasion by his friend Edmund Evans.
John Gilbert also drew some of
the illustrations for these
books. Our artist like-
wise executed for this
firm the illustrations for
Black's Picturesque

Guide to the Trossachs, etc. (1853); *The Shipwreck,*
a poem by William Falconer (1858); *The Grave,*

9

a poem by Robert Blair (1858) ; and *Black's Pic-turesque Guide to the English Lakes* (1858).

The drawings for the engravings for these books were mostly small and represented landscapes, but many had domestic incidents introduced into them and a large number were vignetted.

For nearly all the books Birket Foster made his drawings on wood-blocks, but in a few cases he etched the subjects himself on steel. These were Milton's *L'Allegro and Il Penseroso,* with twenty-nine etchings (1855) ; *The Traveller,* by Oliver Goldsmith, with thirty etchings (1856) ; *The Rhine and its Picturesque Scenery* in two volumes with twenty etchings (1856); all published by Bogue; and *The Hamlet,* by T. Warton, with fourteen etchings (1859), Sampson Low and Co. These dainty etchings are quite small, and are especially interesting as showing his work at that period without the intervention of the engraver. Owing to the hardness of the material on which they were etched they have a resemblance to fine engravings.

At the suggestion of the present writer Birket Foster was induced to make his first etching on copper in the year 1880 for a publication entitled *The Etcher,* as may be seen from the following letter :—

THE HILL, WITLEY, SURREY,
12th April 1880.

DEAR MR. CUNDALL—I tried my hand at an etching, but it is so long since I did anything of that kind, I am rather diffident about sending it to you. I had intended throwing it on one side and trying again, but my painting engagements are so increasing that I fear I shall not have time to do anything more at present, and if you think it will suit you well and good. The printer will be able to do more for it I daresay than you see in this proof.—Believe me, very sincerely yours, BIRKET FOSTER.

I send proof by this post.

Although the first proof of this etching, " Sheep Feeding," was not quite to Foster's satisfaction, he was much pleased with the proofs printed by Mr. Goulding, for in a subsequent letter he says, " I think the printing *admirable*."

The success of this plate naturally brought requests from other publishers for etchings, and Foster, although his time was fully occupied in water-colour painting, was persuaded to execute a few more of them—" An Old Mill " (1881) and " The Little Shepherds" (1890) appeared in *The Art Journal.* He also etched a few other plates, amongst which may be mentioned : " The Wandering Minstrel " (1881), published by Messrs. Dowdeswell ; " Crossing the Brook " (1883), by Messrs. Tooth ; a reproduction of the painting " The Street,

Cookham," by Fred. Walker, A.R.A., for Mr. T. Maclean (1888); and "Home, Sweet Home" (1891), by the Fine Art Society.

After the year 1858 Birket Foster accepted very few engagements for black and white drawings for

MONT ST. MICHEL.

book illustrations, as he was now turning his attention almost solely to water-colour painting. He had, however, agreed with the Dalziel Brothers to make a series of drawings larger than usual to be thoroughly representative of rustic English scenery, and after a lapse of nearly five years Messrs. Routledge and Co. published *Birket Foster's Pictures of English Landscape* in 1863. The illustrations were beautifully engraved by the Dalziels and were accompanied by verses by Tom Taylor and his wife. Many other books were issued after this date containing wood-engravings after drawings by Birket Foster, but in nearly every case they were old blocks which had been used in previous publications. Birket Foster himself published a series of thirty-five views in Brittany, produced by lithography by Messrs. Maclure and Macdonald in 1878, after a recent trip to that part of France. The sketches were drawn on prepared paper and transferred to stone, so that the pictures may be said to have been printed from the actual drawings; and *Some Places of Note in England*, with twenty-five drawings also transferred to stone, with descriptive notes by the artist, was published by Messrs. Dowdeswell in 1888.

TRAVELS ON THE CONTINENT

AMIENS.

CHAPTER V

TRAVELS ON THE CONTINENT

ALTHOUGH the rural scenery of his native country had its peculiar charms for his pencil, still Birket Foster was greatly attracted by the grander views to be obtained on the Continent. His early visits were made to the Rhine, but subsequently the Italian lakes and Venice were his favourite hunting grounds in search for "bits" to sketch. The word "bits" is particularly applicable in the case of Birket

Foster, for he almost invariably preferred to make a drawing of some detail rather than a broad landscape. He used to say that the mountain scenery of Switzerland was too panoramic and had no attractions for him. It is somewhat remarkable that whilst he relied to a great extent on lanes and fields, and hedgerows and rustic children for his English drawings, the views for his Continental paintings were largely selected from towns with architectural details introduced into them.

The first visit made to the Continent by Birket Foster was in 1852, when he was accompanied by Henry Vizetelly, the printer and engraver, and by another companion named Fry.

David Bogue, the publisher, had determined to bring out an illustrated edition of *Hyperion* by Longfellow, and commissioned our artist to follow in the footsteps of Paul Flemming, and to depict on the spot the varied scenes, amid which the poet had laid the incidents of his story. Paul Flemming, as is well known, was Longfellow himself, and the romance a passage in the author's own life.

The result of the journey was nearly one hundred drawings, which were afterwards transferred to wood-blocks and engraved by Vizetelly.

Hyperion with these illustrations was published in the following year, and in a note at the end of the volume Vizetelly, gives particulars of the route taken by them. He says, " Thanks to railways and the power of steam, the morning following our departure from London found us breakfasting by an open window, overlooking the magnificent Rhine, and a few hours afterwards brought us face to face with the ruins of Roland-seck and the Kloster Nonnenwerth." These soon sketched, the Round Tower at Andernach was visited. Next object the Crucifix, known as the " Christ of Andernach," which had formerly stood outside the church, was found after a search inside the building, whither it had been removed some years previously. Sketches of Liebenstein and Ster-nenfels were made from the river, whilst passing by in the steamer. Halts were made at Bingen and Mainz; afterwards Frankfort—Goethe's birth-place, Weinheim and Heidelberg were visited. Thence they proceeded to Switzerland and the Alps, stopping at Interlaken. Continuing in the footsteps of Paul Flemming, they travelled into the Tyrol, and sketches were made at Waidering, "the little white village" of St. Gilgen, and adjacent places. At St. Wolfgang they were rowed in a boat by two peasant women, and passed under the mighty precipice of Falkenstein. Birket Foster and Vizetelly returned by way of Salzburg, Munich, Augsburg, Ulm, and Stuttgart, and reached London after an absence of six weeks, greatly more familiarised with the romance of *Hyperion.*

In the next year Birket Foster travelled through Belgium and up the Rhine, as far as Constance, stopping at many places *en route* to make sketches. He was accompanied on this occasion by his wife and a relative, Dr. R. Spence Watson. The result of this trip was *The Rhine and its Picturesque Scenery,* illustrated by engravings on steel after Foster's drawings and published in two volumes by David Bogue. In October of the year 1859, shortly after the death of his first wife, Birket Foster took his wife's niece, Miss Brown, now Mrs. Edmund Evans, who had nursed her aunt through the fatal illness, a trip through Belgium to the Rhine and back by way of Paris. They were accompanied by Mr. and Mrs. Joseph Cundall, the father and mother of the author of the present volume. At this time Birket Foster and his children were residing at 12 Carlton Hill East, St. John's Wood, and as we lived nearly opposite to them in the same road, an intimacy had sprung

FEEDING TIME

DESIGNS FOR BOOK COVERS

EVENING ON THE YARE

YOUNG GLEANERS RESTING

MANCHESTER CATHEDRAL

STIRLING FROM THE ABBEY CRAIG

CROSSING THE FORD

PASS OF KILLIECRANKIE

up between the two families. Birket Foster and my father were great friends, and the latter brought out numerous illustrated gift-books, so fashionable at that period, the majority of which contained engravings from Birket Foster's drawings.

An account of this tour on the Continent was afterwards written in doggerel rhyme by Joseph Cundall, privately printed as a small *brochure*, with an illustration of the Rhine by Birket Foster, as a frontispiece. It commences with the following lines:—

> We took a cab from Carlton Hill
> (A very sorry hack we had)
> And drove away to Kath'rine's Wharf,
> Where all the scene look'd very sad;
> For round the quays, and o'er the ships,
> A dense smoke-smelling fog there hung.
> And when we got on board our boat
> We scarce could see which way she swung,

and from these verses we learn that they went by steamer from London to Ostend, where they stopped the night. The following morning they were all up at six o'clock and took the train to Bruges; visited the sights in that old town and continued their journey to Ghent. After having explored that place, the next day they proceeded to Antwerp, crossing the Scheldt in a steamboat, as in those days "No bridge was there

across the stream." After visiting Brussels they
went on to Cologne, and thence to Rolandseck, of
which Byron sings—

> And peasant-girls, with deep-blue eyes,
> And hands which offer early flowers,
> Walk smiling o'er this Paradise;
> Above, the frequent feudal towers
> Through green leaves lift their walls of grey,
> And many a rock which steeply lowers,
> And noble arch in proud decay,
> Looks o'er this vale of vintage bowers,

but they were not so fortunate as to meet any
peasant-girls. Here they took the steamboat up
the Rhine past Andernach and Coblenz to St Goar
where

> Bad beds, bad smells, and noises loud
> Keep us awake for many an hour.

Afterwards they continued
their journey up the river
by boat to Mainz. Here
they left the Rhine and
proceeded by the train
to Saarbruck, where they
stopped the night, and on
the following day travelled
by way of Metz and Eper-

ST. GERMAIN, LOOKING SOUTH.

nay to Paris. Here they stayed for some days
and returned home by Boulogne and Folkestone,

Being late in the autumn, the weather was not suitable for out-door sketching, and Birket Foster did very little work.

In the autumn of the following year Birket Foster again travelled over the greater part of the same ground. He started from Newcastle-on-Tyne and was accompanied by his niece, Miss Brown, her uncle and aunt, Mr. and Mrs. Joseph Watson, and Dr. R. Spence Watson. On this occasion the trip was not recorded in verse, but Dr. Watson on his return home contributed no less than sixteen articles entitled " A Three Weeks' Ramble in the Autumn of 1860 " to the *Newcastle Journal*, giving an interesting and detailed diary of all their doings, "recalling the beauties of the Rhine, the glories of Switzerland, and the pleasures of France." The party left Newcastle by steamboat and crossed the North Sea to Rotterdam ; thence went by rail to Dentz, and from Cologne to Coblenz, where they took the steamer up the Rhine to Castel. After visiting Frankfort and Heidelberg they proceeded to Switzerland, stopping at Basle and Lucerne. From the latter place they ascended the Righi; and afterwards crossed the Grimsel to Interlaken. All the party were on horseback with the exception of Dr. Watson, who was a good pedestrian and preferred to trust himself to his own legs. In his narrative in dealing with the mode of progression, he lets a little side-light into Birket Foster's equestrian prowess, as he says "the only drawback to the perfect happiness of the party was the horses. They were certainly quiet animals; but I have always observed that, however excellent in this respect, they can tell immediately whether he who straddles them is accustomed to his position. If he is not, they at once conceive a cool contempt for him, and evince it by looking round in a sneering manner, standing still to eat grass by the wayside; nay, Mr. F.'s brute even went so far as to commence to lie down, and but for the timely assistance of one of the men engaged to look after them, would doubtless have accomplished its intention." They continued their journey to Geneva by way of Berne, Freyburg and Vevay, and afterwards returned home through Macon and Paris. This being a pleasure-trip to see as much as possible in three weeks, Birket Foster had little or no time in which to make many drawings, but his spare moments were always engaged in making pencil notes in one of his sketch-books without which he never travelled.

Birket Foster was again in Switzerland in 1865.

On this occasion he was accompanied by his second wife, whom he had married in the previous year, and Miss S. Edmondson, now Mrs. Heseltine.

S. GIOVANNI, LAKE COMO.

For some time our artist had been desirous of feasting his eyes upon the beauties of Venice, and in the following year Mr. and Mrs. Birket Foster with his niece, Miss E. Brown, now Mrs. Alfred Cooper, and a Mr. Bridger, who acted as his secretary, left England with the full intention of reaching the "Queen of the Adriatic." They travelled through Belgium by way of Ghent and Antwerp to Luxemburg; thence to Treves, where they remained for three days exploring the beauties

11

of that old town. Then down the Moselle to
Coblenz and up the Rhine to Mainz. Next to
Heidelberg and Strassburg, where they stopped during the Whitsuntide to witness the festivities; afterwards through the Black Forest to Schaffhausen
and Zurich; over the Splügen Pass to Bellagio and
Como, and thence to Milan. Here, in consequence
of the Austrian and Italian war, they were not

ARGEGNO.

allowed to proceed any farther, and they had to
abandon all hope of seeing Venice in that year. Nor
could they return home for some little time as the

military authorities would not permit any one to
leave the town lest information as to the move-
ments of the Italian troops might be conveyed to
the enemy.   Eventually, however, our party were
allowed to quit Milan, and they returned home
by the St. Gothard Pass after an absence of six
weeks.

FIRST VISIT TO VENICE

COLICO.

CHAPTER VI

FIRST VISIT TO VENICE

In the early summer of 1868 Birket Foster set off again for Venice and arrived there on this occasion without any *contre-temps*. He was accompanied by Mrs. Foster, Mrs Brown, Miss E. Brown, and Mr. W. Q. Orchardson, R.A. They travelled there through France and returned by way of Switzerland and the Rhine. The following account of their tour is extracted from a diary kept by Mrs. Brown.

11th May, London.—On our arrival at Waterloo

Station from Witley, De Heer, our courier, met us and took charge of all our bags and baggage. We drove to St. James's Restaurant, where Mr. Orchardson was waiting and our dinner ready. We had plenty of time at Charing Cross as our train did not start till 8.30 P.M.

12th May, Calais.—Landed, after a delightful crossing, at 12.30 A.M., and on reaching our hotel found our supper and beds ready. This morning, after looking at the church, market-place, etc, we set out for Paris.

13th May, Paris.—We arrived here yesterday evening by a new route *vid* Boulogne and the coast to Amiens, and went to Meurice's Hotel. After dinner we looked at Paris by gaslight. Directly after breakfast we start for Macon, and to-morrow we hope to sleep at the foot of the Alps.

15th May, Marseilles.—Yesterday we dined at Dijon and reached Macon about 8 o'clock. Here I first saw the pretty lace bed-curtains, of which I had heard so much. This morning we were up at 4 o'clock to catch the train. After we had started Birket gave us a surprise by telling us that Mr. Orchardson and he had changed their plans a little, and that we were going to Marseilles. We stopped at Lyons for a short while, and then passed along for some time amongst vines and groves of mulberries ; next we came to olives and fig-trees and then to a fine river, which I discovered to my surprise was the Rhone. At last the Mediterranean lay before us. The gentlemen had long wished to come this way and found it feasible only when we were in Paris. We reached Marseilles in time for *table-d'hôte*. In the evening we walked about the town, which was very picturesque with the costumes of the Oriental people.

16*th May, Nice.*—Whilst dressing this morning I heard a great commotion in the courtyard, and was greatly amused in watching all the passengers who had just arrived by the Indian mail. Directly after breakfast we drove in an open carriage by the sea, which was intensely blue. At 1 o'clock we again set out by train and passed groves of olives, which went right down to the sea. As we neared Cannes the scenery was magnificent, the mountains at the back were covered with snow, and whilst we passed amongst groves of orange-trees and hedges of roses and geraniums, the air was quite luscious with their scent.

19*th May, Mentone.*—We spent a quiet Sunday at Nice, and yesterday we left there at 10 A.M. in a carriage drawn by four horses, in which we are to

12

drive all the way to Genoa. We soon began to ascend till we were nearly 3000 feet above the sea, and reached a village, where women in such primitive costumes were washing clothes at a fountain. We stayed whilst the two gentlemen made sketches. As we got lower down the vegetation was more wonderful than ever. There were palm-trees, huge aloes, and cacti, whilst the air was redolent with the scent of the lemon-trees, which abounded on every side. We are delighted with this mode of travelling, and as our road lies all the way by the coast, the heat is tempered by the sea breezes, but sometimes blue spectacles are indispensable as everything is so intensely bright.

21st *May, Savona.*—Soon after leaving Mentone we entered Italy, where we left our carriage to walk up a steep hill, whilst the baggage was examined; our courier manages matters so cleverly that not a single box has yet been unlocked. We kept along the high cliffs above the Mediterranean for a long while. The palms and other tropical trees were very fine here, and each day we see some fresh wonder in vegetation. We continued as far as San Remo, where we stopped for the night. After dinner we set out for a walk amongst the fire-flies, which flashed about in every direction. We had not been long at our hotel when Prince Füstenberg, two ladies, and servants drove up to stay the night, and as we had secured the best rooms, they had to be content with the floor above us. The next day's drive was very fine—still along the shores and rocks of the Mediterranean to Alassio, where we slept. We went on the sea-shore in the evening, but were so soon surrounded by a mob of wildly shouting children that we were glad to beat a retreat. The following day we arrived at this place, Savona, where we are stopping the night.

26th May, Venice.—After leaving Savona we reached Genoa, where our wonderful drive along the Corniche Road came to an end, and joined the railway once more, travelling by it to Bologna. Genoa is a very fine city, and the situation is beautiful, but I think we were all more pleased with Bologna. It is a very ancient city, and the churches, paintings, and everything are so fine. We found the narrow streets and colonnades very essential to our comfort. It was so intensely hot that we were glad to set out in the cool of the evening on the last part of our journey to Venice. Here we are really at Venice. No one can form any idea of the grandeur of the place without

really seeing it. My first impressions were those
of awe, for we arrived in the twilight and the
gondolas came stealing past us in such a mysterious
manner. After our baggage had been examined, we
entered our gondolas, and away we went in capital
style, with the gondoliers standing up and making
long sweeps with the oars. It is wonderful how
they escape collisions, as the gondolas are propelled
through such narrow spaces. We soon reached
the Hôtel de l'Europe, and after a late dinner we
felt it impossible to wait until the morning to look
at some of the far-famed places, so we wandered
about till we had seen the Bridge of Sighs and
other sights. We are highly favoured. Owing
to Prince Humbert and his bride being here, the
city wears its very gayest aspect. The following
morning we set out for a general inspection of the
place and were on the water for hours. In the
evening we witnessed the illuminations. St.
Mark's Square was magnificent, and the people
of all nations, tongues, and climes promenading
about made it a wonderful sight. We all agreed
that Venice far exceeded our most sanguine
expectations.

The next evening we saw a most gorgeous
spectacle in honour of the Prince and Princess

LOCHLEVEN CASTLE

DUNFERMLINE ABBEY

HAWTHORNDEN

VENICE FROM THE STEPS OF SAN GIORGIO MAGGIORE

SHRINE AT THE ENTRANCE OF THE COURTYARD OF
THE DUCAL PALACE, VENICE

THE LIBRARY IN THE PIAZZETTA, VENICE

WELL IN THE COURTYARD OF THE DUCAL PALACE, VENICE

IN THE VESTIBULE, ST. MARK'S, VENICE

from the balcony of our hotel. The view was unequalled. First came two immense barges (about twice as large as our steam ferries at North Shields) entirely covered with lamps of every conceivable colour, hung on domes and towers and all over them. These were followed by about three thousand gondolas with every imaginable device of illumination. They all stopped opposite our hotel to serenade, with most exquisite music,

VENICE FROM THE LIDO.

the Prince and Princess who were on board one of the barges; then they all swept away down the Grand Canal, the whole of which was lit up with a blaze of rockets and red and blue lights. I can give no adequate idea of the grandeur of the whole scene.

This morning Birket and Mr. Orchardson went off in the gondola, which we have hired during our stay, in search for subjects to paint, whilst our courier took us ladies into St. Mark's and to look at the shops. I am now writing this diary in the gondola, which is fastened up to enable Birket to sketch, and whilst I write I can hear the Italian National Anthem stealing over the water, as the Prince, who has been to see the fisheries, has just passed us in a steamboat.

I must not forget to mention that we have met Freddy Walker, who has been here a week.

[Frederick Walker, or rather Fred., as he was called by all his friends, in a letter dated 26th May 1868, says :—

"The Fosters and Orchardson are here in this very hotel. Yesterday morning I was coming in to lunch, when I found the whole party on the steps. They had arrived on Sunday night without my knowing anything of it; the other hotel they intended putting up at was full. The Fosters are very jolly and kind, and all going first-rate.[1]]

28th May, Venice.—Yesterday morning was devoted to sight-seeing. We visited the Doge's Palace, the Bridge of Sighs, and other places. After dinner we witnessed a serenade on the Grand Canal. Freddy Walker joined us in our gondola. We got a capital position, so that when Prince Humbert and his bride came out, we were almost close to them. She is a beautiful young creature. It is quite impossible to give any idea of the

[1] *Life and Letters of Frederick Walker, A.R.A.*, by John George Marks,—Macmillan and Co.

gorgeous spectacle. Hundreds of gondoliers were dressed in most magnificent costumes ; some in blue and gold, and some very curiously with one leg red and the other white ; and the gondolas were decked out with the utmost elegance. Then the music commenced, and the whole mass moved gently on, the speed increasing as we went. At the Rialto Bridge the gondola with the Royal party turned, and all the procession went down the Grand Canal again. It was almost dark before we reached our hotel. The whole scene was lit up by coloured lights from the banks and the gondolas around us.

This morning the gentlemen are away at work.

30th May, Venice.—The day before yesterday I went in the morning with Birket in the gondola. We looked into Sta Maria della Salute, and were much pleased with the paintings, particularly "The Marriage in Cana," by Tintoretto, and "The Descent of the Holy Spirit," by Titian. In the evening we all attended a fête in the public gardens, which were wonderfully lit up with lamps of every colour. The Royal party twice passed us closely. The young bride looked so sweet and smiling : she is more lively than her sister, the Queen of Portugal, who has been here with her. Our gondolier, Antonio, kept us in view of the place where they would re-embark, and we had a grand row back to the hotel, keeping alongside the Royal gondola all the way. Yesterday morning the gentlemen were away at work again, and in the afternoon we went with Birket who is sketching down the canal.

31st May.—This being Sunday we went early to St. Mark's. We were just in time to see a cardinal and nine bishops make their entry. The scene was most gorgeous, and the music finer than any we have yet heard; one voice was wonderful. The dressing and undressing of the Cardinal was very curious; his feet were washed with great solemnity; bowing, ringing of bells, and waving of incense went on all the time.

1st June, Venice.—I was up at six o'clock this morning, and joined Birket and Freddy Walker at an early breakfast, after which we went down the lagoon in our gondola to catch a steamboat which was going to Chioggia, a fishing town about twenty miles away on the shores of the Adriatic. We had a lovely voyage and I enjoyed nursing a lovely baby, but it was so queerly swaddled up that it was not easy to keep hold of it. The costumes of the inhabitants of Chioggia are very picturesque. The women wear a garment which looks most becoming; it is like a large muslin apron, put on behind and then thrown over the head, just leaving the face to be seen, many of which are very lovely. We visited a church almost filled with women in these costumes, and also went into the fishmarket. I really did feel a foreigner, and was never so much stared at in my life. The people stood in crowds to look at us. It is a very picturesque place, but so queer and dirty that I was glad to return to the steamboat. The wind had freshened, so we had a brisk voyage on our way back and we reached our hotel in time for *table d'hôte*. During our absence the others had been with Mr. Orchardson on the Lido and had visited numerous churches. Yesterday was devoted to going over churches and the Academy of Fine Arts. The Scalzi is a very gorgeous church. In the evening we were out in the gondola till nearly ten o'clock. It was such a still moonlight night, the reflection of the moon being almost perfectly round.

To-day we have been in the gondola to the Church of the Jesuits, an old disused palace, but still splendid. Now and then we stopped, whilst Birket made some sketches, but he found it impossible to do much work, as the heat was so overpowering.

13

4th June, Venice.—We are all ready to leave here to-morrow morning. Though a little cooler, it is still too hot for any work. This morning we went on the Rialto, then to luncheon at our favourite restaurant, Baur's, and afterwards had a long pull in the gondola to the Lido. We walked across it, and strolled along the sea-shore. The fishing-boats on the Adriatic are most picturesque.

5th June, Verona.—It was quite a pinch for us to leave Venice this morning. The city looked so beautiful as our gondoliers, Angelo and Louis, rowed us down the Grand Canal for the last time. We thoroughly enjoyed our fortnight there.

Freddy Walker left with us.

[Frederick Walker wrote on the 6th June from the Hotel Cavour, Milan:

"I left Venice early yesterday morning with the Fosters, and went with them to Verona. We got there about two, and spent the afternoon in quietly driving about the place. The Fosters had telegraphed for rooms and we were very comfortable. In leaving Venice with them I avoided a world of discomfort, for getting away is notoriously dreadful; the confusion and bother quite maddening at the station, where they are awfully strict in searching all baggage, etc., and although I left the hotel with them I had my own gondola, for poor Antonio would insist upon my being served by himself and the lad up to the last, although I had settled our little matters the night before. So I followed the Fosters up the canals, and tipped the lad through the curtain of the boat. Of course their courier managed everything at the station, and so my departure from Venice was a very different affair from what it might have been, had I left the place alone.

We left Verona this morning, and I took leave of them finally at Bergamo, where they had to change carriages, for they are going to the Lakes, and cross the Alps at St. Gothard, and finish up with the Rhine. They were all very sorry to lose me, I think, and I am sure I was to leave them, for they have been most jolly.]

It seemed very odd once more to come to a region of cabs, omnibuses, and horses again, after not seeing any for so long, but Venice with its three hundred and six waterways has no use for such things. We passed through Padua and Mantua. Some of the distant views were beautiful, both of the Apennines and the Alps; the latter had snow on their summits.

This afternoon we had a drive round the town, and saw some of the churches and an amphitheatre, which is considered more perfect than the Coliseum at Rome though not quite as large. This is the oldest-looking town we have visited, with narrow streets like all Italian towns.

7th June, Bellagio.—We left Verona about 10 A.M., and very soon the country became very hilly. There is a lovely view of Lago di Garda, as the

railway runs along the side of the lake for many
miles. It is the largest of the Italian lakes and
very beautiful. We saw snow in the distance,
where is the highest pass into Switzerland. At
Bergamo we parted company with Freddy Walker,

LECCO, LAKE COMO.

who proceeded to Milan, whilst we turned north-
wards, and on reaching Lecco, we and our baggage
were transferred into a boat and we had a delightful
sail up Lake Como. As we neared Bellagio the
sunset lit up some of the highest peaks, which were
covered with snow. I never saw any water such
a lovely colour as this lake, so green and so
exquisitely clear. I think its beauty can hardly

be exceeded, the rocks being so very fine and clothed down to the water's edge with vines, olives, figs, and other trees.

9th June, Bellagio.—We did not expect to be here still, but for the first time since leaving England

BELLAGIO, LAKE COMO.

we have had stormy weather. We had, however, seen a good deal of this place before it came on. We took a boat to Villa Julia, where are splendid views both up and down the lake; on rowing back we passed close to the rocks to gather maidenhair, which grows down to the water's edge. We went yesterday to see a waterfall, which rushes out of a cavern about half-way up one of the mountains.

As we were returning the wind sprung up and we had a rough passage back to our hotel. Towards the evening the storm increased to a gale with thunder and lightning. We are now storm-bound, as the boats cannot run, and the lake is like an angry sea.

11*th June, Lugano.*—The storm so far abated yesterday that we were able to leave Bellagio and cross the lake in a steamboat to Menaggio with about forty other travellers, several of whom had intended to cross the Splügen or the Simplon Passes, but were obliged to change their routes, as we learnt that a great amount of snow had fallen. To our dismay, on arrival at Menaggio we found that all the carriages had been bespoken, and that we must either walk six miles over the mountains or wait until the afternoon. Mrs. Foster and my daughter at once started off with Mr. Orchardson, Birket and I following not quite decided what to do, when Admiral Lambert and his party overtook us and kindly invited us into their carriage. The road was so hilly that we did not overtake the walkers until they had gone nearly four miles; soon after we had passed them they fortunately met an empty carriage, so we all managed to catch the steamer to Lugano. During the passage another thunderstorm came on with torrents of rain, but it now looks like fine weather again. This is a lovely place and a delightful hotel.

14th June, Lucerne.—Here we are safely over the St. Gothard, after a most pleasant journey. The drive from Lugano to Bellinzona, where we slept the night, was very fine, with beautiful views of Lake Maggiore. We started the next morning at 8 A.M. and stopped to rest the horses at Faido, where there is a grand waterfall. We saw it to the best advantage owing to the recent snowfall on the mountains.

Yesterday we reached Airolo, which is about 4000 feet above the sea. The mountains covered with snow towering above the little village are very grand.

This morning we left at 7 A.M. and commenced climbing St. Gothard at once. We all walked for about two-thirds of the way up. During the descent we left our carriage to walk across the Devil's Bridge. It was magnificent indeed, the scenery all the way being very grand.

We passed through Hospenthal, Armsteg, and Altorf with its statues of William Tell and towers. Here we took the steamboat to Lucerne, which we reached in about two hours, all very tired after twelve hours travelling through such exciting scenery.

It is so very nice to settle down for a quiet Sunday here in such delightful rooms in the most perfect of hotels.

18th June, Heidelberg.—After a peaceful Sunday, which was most refreshing, the next morning we looked about Lucerne, and went on to Zurich.

STRESA.

Here we spent the evening in a boat on the lake. It was so beautiful and still that we were reminded of our evenings at Venice. On Tuesday we left for Schaffhausen, where we visited the falls, which were wonderfully fine owing to the recent snow. Yesterday we had a long day's journey to Strassburg.

This morning we wandered about the town; some of the old parts are very picturesque, and the storks flying about or seated on the chimneys give the place a very peculiar appearance. We saw the wonderful clock performance at noon, when the twelve apostles came out and bowed, and the cock crew thrice. What a beautiful tower and spire to the cathedral, but it is difficult to believe it is more than one hundred feet higher than our St. Paul's. We reached here (Heidelberg) in time for dinner.

Here the diary ends. After leaving Heidelberg the party went down the Rhine, stopping at Coblenz and Cologne, and thence back to England by way of Ghent.

FURTHER TRAVELS ON THE CONTINENT

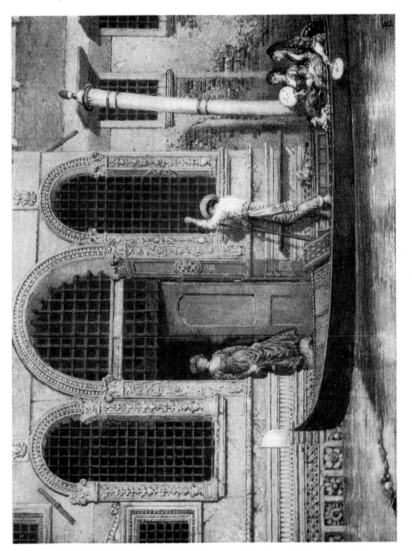

PALAZZO GUSSONI, VENICE

BURANO, VENICE

ENTRANCE TO THE GRAND CANAL, VENICE

PISA

BIRTHPLACE OF BURNS, NEAR AYR

A HIGHLAND COTTAGE

BEN VENUE AND ELLEN'S ISLE, LOCH KATRINE

LICHFIELD CATHEDRAL

COMO.

CHAPTER VII

FURTHER TRAVELS ON THE CONTINENT

In 1869 Messrs. Moxon and Co. arranged to
publish an illustrated edition of Hood's *Poems*,
and commissioned Birket Foster to make the
necessary drawings, which were afterwards beautifully engraved on steel by William Miller, who at
that time was nearly eighty years of age. For this
purpose Birket Foster visited Belgium, Holland, and
the Rhine, and as he always preferred to have companions with him during these tours abroad—in fact
he never went on the Continent alone—he was

accompanied by his eldest son Myles, and his friend Alfred Cooper, the son of Abraham Cooper, R.A.

On this occasion they naturally went *viâ* Ostend where Hood resided for nearly three years, from May 1837 to the spring of 1840, when he returned to England. From there the party travelled to Bruges, Ghent, and Antwerp; next they went to Rotterdam, where Hood landed in 1835. They made excursions from here to The Hague, Amsterdam, and other towns in Holland; afterwards went up the Rhine to Coblenz, and Birket Foster made sketches for Hood's poem " Up the Rhine," which the poet wrote during his residence of two years in that town.

Our artist was no great linguist, and often failed to grasp the meaning of a foreigner's attempt at the English language. Mr. Cooper narrates that whilst they were at dinner on one occasion at a German hotel, the proprietor, noticing that Birket Foster was not relishing a beefsteak which had been dished up with sauce and various flavourings, approached him and said in broken English, " To-morrow the bifstek shall be cooked in the best English manner." Birket Foster looked puzzled and inquired of Cooper what the fellow meant by wanting to cook a steak in English *manure.*

In 1874, having a commission to paint a series of pictures at Venice, Birket Foster again travelled on the Continent. This time his companions were Robert Dudley, the artist, and Captain Frank Coleridge. They left London on 11th May and went by way of Ostend and Brussels to Spa, where they stopped for some days on a visit to Monsieur E. Gambart, the well-known London picture-dealer at that time, who had a country residence near to the town.

On leaving Spa they went to Cologne, and up the Rhine through Alsace, stopping to sketch at Strassburg, Basle, Laufenburg, Schaffhausen ; then down to Lucerne and to Villeneuve and Chillon on the Lake of Geneva, up the valley of the Rhone and over the Simplon Pass to Stresa on Lago Maggiore. After stopping there for a short time the party proceeded by way of Milan to Venice. Here a long stay was made to enable the two artists to paint many subjects. They had intended afterwards to visit Florence, but the weather became so hot that they directed their steps homewards, making a short stop at Verona, then over the St. Gothard Pass to Zurich, and by Basle to Paris.

In the next year, 1875, Birket Foster was again

in Venice to complete many of the drawings commenced in the previous year, and also to find
numerous other irresistible subjects.   On this
occasion he took his second son William, and
Robert Dudley again was one of the party.   They

COLICO, LAKE COMO.

went by the Riviera and Genoa, and returned by
Milan to Lake Como, making a long stay at Bellagio
to sketch in the neighbourhood.   They met with
a carriage accident on the hills above Menaggio on
the opposite side of the lake, but fortunately no
one was seriously hurt.   Thence they proceeded
over the St. Gothard Pass to Lucerne, staying at
the Schweizerhof Hotel, where more sketches were

made, then home by Basle and Paris as in the previous year.

During the summers of 1876 and 1877 Birket Foster made two sketching tours in Normandy and Brittany. He was accompanied by Robert Dudley

MONT ST. MICHEL.

on both occasions, and by his friends, Captain F. Coleridge in 1876, and Captain C. Nelson, R.N., in 1877. The latter was Captain of H.M.S. *Galatea* when the King, then Prince of Wales, and his brother, the late Duke of Coburg, visited Australia. On the first trip they left England on 20th May, and Amiens was their first halting-place.

15

From there they went to Beauvais and Rouen,
then to Honfleur, Caen, Falaise, Avranches, and
Mont St. Michel, where they stayed some time
making numerous sketches. Afterwards they proceeded farther west to St. Malo, Dinan, and

ROUEN.

Quimper.   Next they directed their steps south-
ward to Nantes, and up the river Loire, stopping at
Angers, Saumur, Tours, Amboise, and Blois.   From
the last town they returned home through Paris.

The second trip was commenced on the 30th July in the following year, and the first stay of the little party was at Rouen, and the next at Caen. From there they went to the small town of Vitré and stopped at a quaint hotel which was formerly a country residence of Madame de Sévigné. Afterwards they visited Dol, Guingamp, Morlaix and Quimper. The return voyage to England was made by way of St. Malo and Southampton.

The result of these two sketching tours was the book on Brittany already mentioned, which Birket Foster himself published at The Hill, Witley, in 1878. It consisted of thirty-five sketches made at Vitré, Morlaix, Quimper, Pont l'Abbé, Dol, Dinan, and St. Malo, which were reproduced by lithography. In the preface to the work Birket Foster states: "I have been induced to publish this series of sketches in the hope that it may be acceptable as the exact reproduction of my drawings made in a recent tour in Brittany. A prepared paper was used, and Messrs. Maclure and Macdonald by their delicate process transferred the sketches to stone, so that the pictures in the volume may be said to be printed from the actual drawings. . . . They were not drawn with a view to publication, but were merely the jottings of a rambler in some of the picturesque old towns of that picturesque country." The volumes were dedicated to "my two friends, Captain C. Nelson, R.N., and Robert Dudley, without their permission."

THE MARKET PLACE, ROUEN.

In the spring of the year 1883 Birket Foster made a visit to Spain and Morocco. He, with William, his second son, and Robert Dudley, took the Peninsular and Oriental Steamship *Rohilla*, on the 2nd of April, to Gibraltar. Here, they were detained a week owing to bad weather in the Straits

preventing them from crossing to Tangier, but they
were most hospitably entertained during their enforced stay by the Governor, Sir John Adye, and
his family. Eventually they were able to cross in a
tug-boat, and they put up at Broussaud's Hotel, just
outside the town beyond the camel-market. Here
the party remained for some time making many
sketches, the bright colours of the barbaric costumes affording many subjects for Birket Foster's
pencil. On their return to Gibraltar they took a
steamboat to Cadiz, and from there they went by
train to Seville, where a stay of some days was made.
Thence to Granada to see the Alhambra. Here
Birket Foster made many sketches, and on one day
he climbed up the building to copy some Moorish
ornament, but he was obliged to abandon it, saying
that he thought Moresque patterns must have
been the invention of the devil. Robert Dudley
states that this was the only occasion on which
he ever saw him fail to accomplish a task he
had set himself to do with his pencil. From
Granada the party proceeded to Cordova, thence to
Madrid; afterwards to Avila and Burgos. From
the latter town Birket Foster wrote the following letter, on 26th May 1883, to his eldest son
Myles :—

We have had a most delightful trip. I say *have*, for we are coming home at full speed. Granada is perfect. The Alhambra, the woods full of nightingales, the glorious background of snow mountains, a good hotel and nice people make a thing not to be forgotten. Tangier was another delight. Moors, Arabs, Jews, camels, mosques—no mosquitos —and a good hotel with Arab waiters, the hotel being the only European thing in the place. The music awful. We went to a café to hear Moorish songs, and we did not get over it for days. Gib. was nice, and the Governor, Sir John Adye, and his family also. Seville was wet, and in consequence we did not see much life, but we went to a café and saw gypsies doing fandangos and singing awful ditties—so long that Dudley said he was sure it was the 119th Psalm.

After Seville came Granada, then Cordova with its fine mosque. A magnificent looking organ at Seville, but very brassy ; singing nothing much—beautiful mantillas, kneeling, etc. Cordova organ very fine and well played. From Cordova to Madrid, a Spanish Paris. On Sunday we went to a bull fight. The King and Queen were there. Oh, my goodness ! of all the beastly exhibitions of cruelty. . . . There was such a squash of humanity I couldn't get out, or I shouldn't have been there long. One light-coloured bull went at a horse and man and buried and wriggled his horns in the inside of the horse, emerging with a head bright crimson, the entire inside of the horse hanging down to to the ground, and yet the poor thing stood a minute before he toppled over dead. There are men to stop up small holes with wadding—but oh ! never again so long as I live. From Madrid we went to Toledo ; charming old place. Inn of a very primitive character. After dinner we sat in the old courtyard amongst the diligences. The landlord and his wife also, while the chambermaids danced to the guitars of two blind men for the amusement of the guests. Even the stout landlady danced (castanets of course) a real bit of old Spanish. Organ at Toledo and singing very fine. Back to Madrid to see the Corpus Christi fête. Magnificent procession. Madrid to Burgos, almost the best of all. We leave to-morrow for San Sebastian and so into France.

Myles Foster, having taken up the musical profession and become organist at the Foundling

FLORENCE—IN THE BOBOLI GARDENS.

Hospital, his father naturally refers in his letter to a subject which he knows will interest his son; but, in addition to this, Birket Foster himself was very fond of hearing good music, especially on the organ, hence he was attracted by the musical performances in the various cathedrals which he visited.

From Burgos the travellers crossed over the

Santillanos range of mountains to San Sebastian
and Fuentarabia; then over the Bidassoa into
France, stopping a short time *en route* at San Jean
de Luz and Biarritz, and then home by way of
Bordeaux and Paris, after an absence of two months.

Birket Foster made many subsequent trips to
the Continent, especially to Italy; and from Bellagio
he wrote, on the 15th May 1887: "We are having
very cold weather here at the Lakes. I hope it
won't last, as we have had a good roasting at
Naples and Sorrento. I suppose we shall be
here for a few days more, then move to Lago
Maggiore."

GRAVEDONA, LAKE COMO.

WATER-COLOUR PAINTING

PARIS—PONT NEUF, LOOKING EAST.

CHAPTER VIII

WATER-COLOUR PAINTING

As has already been stated, Birket Foster abandoned the production of pencil-drawings for wood-engravings shortly after the year 1858, and devoted himself almost entirely to water-colour painting.

Like most children, he must have had a box of paints in his young days, for there are still in existence some very early attempts at painting when he was not more than five years old. The dainty water-colour drawing of "The Christmas Holly Cart," executed in 1848, shows that he was no novice at that time, whilst the two views of

123

Tynemouth and Cullercoats and of Arundel Park, as well as the coloured sketch of children, rapidly made on the inside of a used envelope, at Littlehampton, were certainly executed sometime before the year 1858. The sketch and finished drawing of "The Milkmaid" were painted in the Hampstead fields, whilst he was still residing at Carlton Hill East, and his niece, Mrs. Evans, well remembers standing as a model for it.

Birket Foster received little or no instruction in water-colour painting, and in later years when he was frequently pestered by persons asking him to give them lessons in painting, he used to say that he never received any lessons, so he never gave them, believing the best instruction to be obtained from studying the great masters. He was a profound admirer of Turner and Clarkson Stanfield, and it is probable that he was more influenced by the latter's works than by those of any other artist, especially with regard to composition. He delighted to surround himself with paintings by these and other artists in his home at Witley, to which we shall have occasion to refer later.

With regard to his method of working, Birket Foster's early training, as has been seen, was almost exclusively directed towards drawing for wood-

AT QUIMPER

MARKET-PLACE, ROUEN

BURGOS

THE WAY DOWN THE CLIFF

SUNSET WITH CATTLE

CHILDREN PADDLING

COWSLIP GATHERERS

IN FULL CRY

engraving, and it considerably influenced his later, almost entirely water-colour work, which was very dissimilar to the "wash" methods of the early school of water-colour painters. Birket Foster, indeed, worked with his brush as dry as it well could be, and probably no artist in using the medium of water-colours ever used so little water. Of course all painting may be said to be drawing with a brush, but Birket Foster's was practically drawing to a peculiar degree, not washing with a brush. He used a very fine brush with very little paint in it, and owing to his habit of frequently putting it between his lips to make the point of it as fine as possible, it used to be said that the paint came out of the artist's head.[1]

He usually used thick solid cardboards to work on ; those which were called Chalon-boards, after the once popular artist J. Chalon, were very con-

[1] The foregoing remarks refer more particularly to the stippling method which he employed in finishing most of his paintings. In the early drawings, such as "Arundel Park," "Tynemouth," "Cullercoats," and the little sketch produced on an envelope, the colour was freely washed on ; also in the two unfinished figure subjects and a later sketch of Witley Church a full brush was evidently used ; whilst the charming little moonlight effect at sea, rapidly produced by a few lines of Chinese white on a blue ground, belongs quite to the Impressionist School.

venient to pack when travelling, or to carry in a sketching bag, and there was no anxiety in straining paper.

Birket Foster worked very rapidly in his own way of obtaining the effects he desired, and his remarkable gift for composition enabled him to people his scenes with wonderful facility and felicity.

With regard to the vexed question of body-colour —that old artistic tilting arena—Birket Foster was too good a free lance to hold other than broad and liberal views. Although a " purist " in the use of transparent colour, he could yet admit, under any necessity, the useful means of recovering the paper without injuriously soaking and rubbing and sponging the surface into roughness. But he used body-colour, when at all, very sparingly, being nevertheless a most appreciative admirer of the work of Fred. Walker, A.R.A., who certainly must have held very practically that the artist should be the best judge of how or by what means he himself can, or may, best obtain the effects for which he is striving ; and that whatever may be the case in ethics, or at all events in art, the end justifies the means.

It may be said that Birket Foster never engaged

a professional model ; his children were all sketched from the rustic boys and girls whom he found in the course of his wanderings, whilst in the earlier days when he was accustomed to paint what may perhaps be called figure subjects, Mrs. Evans and her sister Mrs. Cooper stood for him, as, for example, in the illustrations *Gleaners* and *Going Home.*

It was at this period that he aspired to be connected with the Old Water-Colour Society, and in the autumn of 1858 he became a candidate for associateship and submitted three drawings with that view, but the minute stippling style, which he had acquired, was not appreciated on this occasion, and he was not successful in being elected. He received, however, some compensation by having a small water-colour painting " A Farm: Arundel Park in the Distance," hung on the walls of the Royal Academy in the spring of the following year.

In 1860 Birket Foster was unanimously elected an Associate of the Old Water-Colour Society, and became a full member two years afterwards. He greatly appreciated the honour which had been conferred upon him, and thoroughly gave his best interests to the Society. In the spring of 1863 he came up from Witley and stopped at the Bedford Hotel to hang the paintings for that year. In a letter dated 14th April 1863, he wrote to Miss Brown—

The first day's work is over, thank goodness. I am nearly worn off my legs; however, I think we have got on tolerably well. I found my companions very agreeable, and we have had great fun; we dined in the Haymarket together. This evening I have been to see Holland, who has sent such a lovely drawing that I went up directly and bought it—one of the finest he has ever done. We invited the President to come and see where we had placed his drawing, for he cannot come without our permission. We have been most bothered with Carl Haag's drawing—a most uninteresting one, like London in a fog; the subject is the Ruins of Palmyra; it has taken us half a day to hang it. Hang it! We meet at breakfast to-morrow at eight for another hard day.—Yours,

B. F.

Three days later he added :—

We have done hanging, and to-morrow we are going to put the finishing touches to it, and to hang a few others we have got as the gallery is not full. If I have not mentioned getting the letters, it has been that from utter prostration after my work, I have hardly known what I have been about.

B. F.

Birket Foster was a most prolific worker, and beside the large number of water-colour paintings exhibited at the Old Society, of which a list is given at the end of this book, many of his drawings were bought by the picture-dealers straight from his studio, and in some cases he received direct commissions for paintings from collectors. Sir Charles Seeley possesses a very fine collection of forty-four Venetian sub-jects, reproductions of six of which are given in this volume. They were all commissioned by the owner's father, and have never been exhibited to the public.

In 1882 Messrs. J. and W. Vokins held a special loan exhibition of Birket Foster's drawings at their establishment in Great Portland Street, at which one hundred and eighteen examples were shown; and in 1896 Messrs. Tooth exhibited a series of Scottish scenes, which Birket Foster executed specially for that firm.

Whilst Birket Foster was residing at Witley, his water-colour paintings became so popular that there was a rush made by the dealers to secure them. *À propos* of this, an amusing story is told, how the

17

principals of two well-known art firms were on the
platform of Waterloo Station waiting for the train
to take them to Godalming. In those days some
of the trains ran only as far as the terminus station,
Old Godalming, now used entirely for goods traffic.
A. catching sight of B., and knowing that there
were but few public vehicles to be hired at Godalming, telegraphed to secure one before entering the
train. On arrival at their destination, B., who had
seen A., immediately jumped out and rushed to
secure the only carriage at the station, but to his
disappointment, he found it was already engaged.
Shortly afterwards A. sauntered up and exclaimed,
" Holloa, B., you here ! If you are going to Witley,
can I give you a lift ? " The offer was readily
accepted, but as soon as they had started off together
A. made it a stipulation that he should have first
visit to the studio. It is needless to add that B.
did not obtain many drawings on that occasion.

Another story is told showing the phenomenal
demand for Birket Foster's drawings. It is said that
on one occasion at a private view of the Old Water-
Colour Society, when the doors were opened there
was an immediate rush made by the dealers for the
screen on which his drawings were hung, but whilst
they were making their selections, one of them

quietly walked up to the secretary's desk and purchased the whole screen of drawings.

Accounts have been given of numerous visits which Birket Foster made to the Continent in search of subjects to paint, but it would be impossible in one volume to present an adequate description of all the numerous tours he made in the different parts of England and Scotland. He rarely, even in his own country, travelled alone; his genial disposition was adverse to solitude. His comrade Edmund Evans, who has already been mentioned, went on many of his early tours with him and considered them to be the greatest treats of his life; and Robert Dudley, his fellow-artist and companion on many later trips, says, "Any one who knew Birket Foster intimately, and as an artist, would know how indefatigably and steadily he worked; he would also know that his geniality and quick perception of the humorous in any social surroundings was so simple-hearted and

genuine as to render any travels made in his friendly company full of delight and charm. Add the artistic element and they became seasons of joyful anticipation and happiest realisation. So they were to me, and are still so in retrospect."

The sketch-books, of which Birket Foster was never without one in his pocket, were filled with many charming little sketches; a few of them are reproduced in the text of this volume. No less than sixty-eight of these small books were sold at Christie's after his death, and in addition there was a considerable number retained for distribution amongst his family. With regard to the former it is to be regretted that some of the rapid sketches in colour in these books have fallen into the hands of unscrupulous persons, who have caused them to be faked up into finished drawings and have sold them as originals.

As may be seen by glancing through the titles of his exhibited paintings, the neighbourhood around Witley had a great charm for Birket Foster, and drawings made on Hambledon Common and in the village of Chiddingfold, with their picturesque cottages roofed with thatch or red tiles, now fast disappearing, and their leafy lanes with happy children gathering wild-flowers, or the beautiful view from his own residence overlooking the Surrey Weald, with Hindhead and Blackdown in the distance and glimpses of the Brighton Downs beyond, are most appreciated by the public and it is by these paintings he is best known.

"Aldworth," on Blackdown, the home of the late Lord Tennyson, was no great distance from Witley, and it is not surprising that there should have been a friendship between the poet and the artist. The last occasion on which they met was at Fresh-  water, where Tennyson was residing shortly before his death. Whilst walking together they discussed various phases of art, and Tennyson put the following question to Birket Foster: "Why do you painters always prefer a tumble-down cottage to others?" "Because no one likes an unbroken line," was the artist's reply.

Birket Foster, paid many visits to Scotland, and when his children grew up he was accompanied by various members of his family. In the summer of 1869 Myles Foster went with his father on one of these sketching tours. They visited on their way Ely, Grantham, Lincoln, York, and Durham. After stopping a few days at the artist's native town, North Shields, they continued their journey to Melrose, Abbotsford, and Edinburgh. At Lanark he painted the Falls of the Clyde, and afterwards sketched Dunblane Cathedral. A halt was made at Pitlochry, which was a favourite centre, and here Birket Foster converted a cottage opposite to Fisher's Hotel into a studio. Whilst there he made a large water-colour painting of the Falls of the Tummel. On one occasion, whilst he was at work at the Falls, Archdeacon Thorpe, coming to the opposite bank to inquire how he was progressing, slipped and nearly fell into the water. Birket Foster, with his keen sense of humour, immediately shouted out, "Holloa! the Church in danger"—a popular cry at the time owing to the demonstrations of the ritualistic party. Afterwards he painted another lovely subject of the bridge at Clunie, and then returned through the Trossachs.

Birket Foster was also fond of the scenery of the Thames, and during the next summer he was staying at "Black Pots," a house on almost an island just below Windsor railway bridge, when

Fred. Walker sent the following amusing sketch in a letter to Myles Foster, in which he says, " Your description of your own favoured isle is indeed refreshing, especially that referring to the number and quality of crabs caught by certain members of your family, but their recent *nautical*

experience has been great." The fish is supposed to represent Freddy himself, " Well, I never," being one of his favourite expressions. Black Pots, as Walker says, was a " favoured isle," and Birket Foster stayed there with his family on more than one occasion in order to make sketches on the silvery Thames.

Although Birket Foster was not what may be

termed a seascape artist, he was fond of making drawings of children playing on the sea-shore. Later in life he revisited many of the watering-places which he depicted for *The Illustrated London News* in his early days, and instead of sketches for wood-blocks, he painted many charming little scenes like *The Way down the Cliff*.

One of his last visits to the coast was in 1894, when he went for the benefit of his health to Southwold, the favourite resort of Charles Keene and his friend Edwin Edwards, before the diminutive branch line, which now connects the little town with the main line of the Great Eastern Railway, was constructed.

Another phase of Birket Foster's art was his love for painting fruit and flowers. He was greatly attracted by William Hunt's work, and his drawing-room at Witley was adorned by eight of the latter's pictures. As may be expected, the same stippling in Hunt's paintings appears in Foster's works; but whilst the former nearly always painted his fruit pieces the same size as in nature, the latter produced almost miniature representations of them. In fact, most of his water-colour drawings were very small, and amongst the illustrations of his work in this book many of them are the exact size of the originals, and it is marvellous how he could put so much detail in such small draw- ings as "The Market Place, Rouen," "Pisa," or "Burgos," between pp 108–9, and 124–5.

Birket Foster painted a few large landscapes in water- colours. "The Meet," belonging to Mr. Barnet Lewis, is one of the largest; it measures $59\frac{1}{2}$ inches by $27\frac{1}{4}$ inches. See illustration between pp 140–1. There was not, however, the same demand for them as for the smaller ones, which were more suitable for his style of painting; besides, from a commercial point of view, they were not so successful. During the past summer four large pictures, about 46 inches by 30 inches each, entitled "Near Dalmally," "Loch Maree," "Ben Nevis," and "The Market- Place, Verona," were sold at Christie's for £2010, thus averaging about £500 each; whilst at the same sale a small painting, "The Hayfield," measur- ing only 9 inches by $14\frac{1}{2}$ inches, fetched one hundred

18

and seventy-five guineas, or more than three and a half times the price in comparison as to size.

As the pockets of many who were ardent admirers of Birket Foster's art were not sufficiently deep to completely cover his drawings with sovereigns in order to acquire them, the art publishers naturally sought means to bring out reproductions, as nearly like the originals as possible, to meet the public demand, and many of his paintings were reproduced with great fidelity by means of chromo-lithography. In 1874 a charming set of twelve, entitled "Gems of Art by Birket Foster," were chromo-lithographed by Thomas Kell, and published by G. P. M'Queen, and Messrs. Rowney and Co., issued from time to time many single reproductions by the same means of our artist's most favourite subjects. Messrs. Vincent Brooks, Day, and Sons, and other lithographers also printed many excellent copies. Some critics have complained that Birket Foster's own work was too much like chromo-lithography, which was an unjust inversion of the case, the fact being the reproductions were made as like the originals as possible.

Five-and-twenty years ago these chromo-lithographs were most popular, and so admirably produced that they were often mistaken for the original

drawings.   On one occasion Birket Foster himself
failed at a casual glance to detect the difference.
He had sold a small drawing to a private individual,
who, he thought, wished to keep it to hang on his
own walls.   Some time after-
wards, whilst walking in the
Strand, he noticed what he
supposed to be this drawing
in a shop window.   Curiosity
led him into the shop to inquire the price of it, and on
asking the shopman how much
was the Birket Foster drawing
displayed in the window, the
man explained that it was only a chromo-litho-
graph.

The number of these chromo-lithographs led
persons to copy them and afterwards sell them as
drawings by Birket Foster, who was continually
worried by paintings being submitted to him with
inquiries as to their genuineness, so much so that
he was at last compelled to charge a fee of a
guinea ; but still these inquiries did not cease,
and, in order to try and stop this nefarious practice
of forging his works and signature, he registered
his monogram ⌖ , but without avail.

Although Birket Foster painted a large number
of his drawings direct from Nature, still he produced
many of them in his studio, which at Witley was
the first room on the left side of the entrance hall.
This had only an ordinary window, overlooking

FALAISE.

a bank of wild-flowers, which were not allowed to
receive any attention from the gardener. Here
Birket Foster frequently worked close to the window, but he had such a love for his work that not
infrequently in the evening he would paint in the
drawing-room surrounded by his family, with a
drawing on his knees. He used a restricted

CHILDREN BY THE SEA

SUMMER TIME

WINDSOR LOCK

ETON COLLEGE

BY THE THAMES

THE MEET

WITLEY CHURCH

(A sketch)

COTTAGE AT WHEELER STREET, WITLEY

palette, and knew his colours so well that he could
work by lamplight.

After the addition had been made to " The Hill "
at Witley, Birket Foster, like many other water-
colour artists, turned his attention to painting in oils,
and used the billiard room, which had been erected
as a studio.   For the nine years, 1869 to 1877, he
regularly contributed oil-paintings, fourteen in all,
to the Exhibitions at the Royal Academy, but after
that period Birket Foster abandoned this medium,
as he found that his little water-colour gems were
far more appreciated by the public.

In 1876 Foster was elected a member of the
Royal Academy of Berlin, an honour which he
greatly appreciated.

AT WITLEY

CHARTRES.

CHAPTER IX

AT WITLEY

WHEN Birket Foster abandoned the drawing on wood-blocks for book illustrations, and took seriously to water-colour painting, he at first selected his subjects from the fields about Hampstead and Highgate. He soon, however, wandered farther afield, and was attracted by the picturesque scenery of Surrey. During his wanderings in this delightful county he found himself at Witley, near Godalming, and he resolved to have a residence there.

145

It cannot be said that Witley was "discovered" by Birket Foster, for other artists were there before him. J. C. Hook, R.A., had already built himself a residence and studio upon an eminence with a beautiful view overlooking the Weald of Surrey, and on an adjoining piece of land that early promotor of art education and founder of the Victoria and Albert Museum, then called the "Brompton Boilers," Sir Henry Cole, K.C.B., had erected a quaint house with an inscription running round it. There can, however, be no doubt that the genial disposition and the liberal hospitality of the owner of "The Hill" afterwards attracted many of his fellow-artists to the neighbourhood.

Witley station stands at a spot where the railway emerges from a deep cutting with pine woods on either side, and at this period there were but few houses or even cottages in the vicinity, for the village itself lies a mile and a quarter to the northward; but Birket Foster managed to secure the possession of a picturesque cottage called "Tigbourne," situated by the corner of the road leading to Hambledon at the foot of Wormley Hill, and resided there during the summer months.

The accompanying illustration shows the cottage as it was at that time, being reproduced from a photograph taken shortly after he had obtained possession of it. Birket Foster may be seen standing near the entrance; at his side is his niece Miss Brown (Mrs. Edmund Evans), who acted as a mother to his young children after his first wife's death, whilst seated within the porch are her sister, Miss E. Brown (Mrs. Alfred Cooper), and Mrs. Cundall, the mother of the present writer. In the background may be discerned the heads of the five young Fosters, three boys and two girls, lying full length on the lawn.

Birket Foster became so pleased with the neighbourhood that he determined to take up his permanent abode at Witley. After lengthy negotiations, he secured the beautiful site, between Wormley Hill and the railway station, on which he eventually erected a house, and finally quitted St. John's Wood. The land being more extensive than his requirements demanded, later on he disposed of a portion of it to Edmund Evans, who also built himself a home;

thus these two comrades further cemented their
life-long friendship by becoming close neighbours
to each other.

Birket Foster was practically his own architect,
and residing near by he was enabled personally
to superintend the erection of the entire building.
In order that its newness should not offend the
artistic eye, he purchased as many weather-worn
tiles off the old cottages in the neighbourhood
as possible, and placed them on the roof of his
house.   A great amount of care was bestowed
on the internal decorations.   William Morris was
consulted, and Burne-Jones painted seven canvases
illustrating the legend of St. George and the
dragon, which formed a frieze round three sides
of the dining-room.   This interesting series of
pictures are very fine examples of the painter's
early work.   They represent—1st, The King's
daughter walking in her garden ; 2nd, The petition
of his people to the King to free the land from the
ravages of the dragon ; 3rd, The drawing of the lot
as to which of the maidens of the land should be
sacrificed to the dragon, and showing how the
choice falls on the King's daughter; 4th, The
King's daughter, followed by her companions, led
out to sacrifice ; 5th, The Princess left tied to a

BIRKET FOSTER.
From a private photograph.

TIGBOURNE COTTAGE, WITLEY, 1862.

From a private photograph.

DISTANT VIEW OF "THE HILL," WITLEY, WHEN FIRST BUILT.

CHRISTMAS FESTIVITIES.   BIRKET FOSTER AND FRIENDS IN SIXTEENTH CENTURY COSTUME.

From a private photograph.

tree ; 6th, The dragon slain, and the Princess delivered by St. George ; and 7th, The Princess led home, amidst rejoicings of the people. Four of these paintings, now the property of Mr. C. S. Goldman, were shown at the Old Masters' Exhibition at the Royal Academy at the beginning of the present year.

Birket Foster also possessed a large screen of eight folds, upon which were sixteen events of the life of St. Frideswide painted by Burne-Jones. These scenes have since been reproduced in the windows of Christ Church Cathedral at Oxford.

Burne-Jones was also commissioned to make many other designs for adornment of "The Hill,"and numerous reminiscences of this great painter may still be found in various parts of the house. Around the fireplace in the room next to the billiard-room are decorated tiles with the following legend : "This is the story of the maid with the shoe of glass, and how she became Queen that was before called Cinder Wench." In the bedrooms are similar tiles illustrating fairy tales, one set representing "A certain prince who delivered a King's daughter from sleep of a hundred years, wherein she and all hers had been cast by enchantment," and another "How a prince, who by enchantment was under the form of a beast, became a man again by the love of a certain maiden." Many of the windows in both the sitting-rooms and bedrooms, as well as in the passages and on the staircases, are decorated with panels of stained glass by Burne-Jones, those representing "Painting," "Architecture," "Music," and "Sculpture" being specially characteristic works of this painter. In some of the rooms the upper lights of the windows are inscribed with musical scores of madrigals and carols. These were carried out at the suggestion of Charles Keene, a frequent visitor, so that at any moment the occupants, feeling inclined, could break out into part-singing without the trouble of searching for books.

Birket Foster was no egotist, and did not believe in the beauty of his own paintings alone, but was a great admirer and collector of his brother-artists works; consequently the walls of "The Hill" were adorned by many pictures. Amongst them may be mentioned—"A Pastoral Scene," boys tending sheep, and "The Barley Harvest," both specially painted for Birket Foster by J. Linnell, senior; "Venice: Under the Rialto" and "Venice," by James Holland; "The Mendicant," the interior of a Turkish house, and "The Harem," by J. F. Lewis, R.A.; "The Morning of Life," by Sam. Palmer; "The Princess and the Ploughman," by G. J. Pinwell; four small drawings by Millais, and eight by William Hunt, including "May Blossom and Eggs," "Primroses," and "Wild Rose and Egg," all specially painted for the owner. A work entitled "The Chaplain's Daughter," by Frederick Walker, A.R.A., was greatly prized by him. The gems, however, of his collection were a series of eight drawings by Turner, over which he was never tired of revelling, including "Sidon," engraved in the Bible Series, "In the Rhone Valley," "Luxemburg," and "Ehrenbreitstein."

There was also a set of panels, representing scenes from nursery rhymes, by H. S. Marks, R.A. These were originally executed for Joseph Cundall, who issued a series of children's books of rhymes illustrated by Marks, G. D. Leslie, R.A., J. D. Watson, and others.

Marks likewise painted seven panels with gold backgrounds, representing Shakespeare's Seven Ages, for the summer-house at "The Hill."

Birket Foster had a great admiration for blue and white porcelain, and was fortunate in acquiring many fine specimens, some being obtained from the collection of D. G. Rossetti, at reasonable prices, before the craze for collecting had set in and made it almost prohibitive excepting to millionaires to procure the finest examples. He was also a bibliophile, and his library contained many early editions. The illustration between pp. 148–9 shows "The Hill" as it was when first finished, but its hospitable owner soon found the accommodation too limited for entertaining

THE SEINE—SEVRES FROM ST. CLOUD.

his many friends. Accordingly in the year 1866 considerable alterations were made. An addition with a large gable was erected at the east end of the house, and a billiard-room beyond it. In the latter J. D. Watson commenced two large frescoes in white and gold, "The Feast of the Peacock" and "The Raising of the Maypole," but they were never completed.

As the name of the house implies, it stands on a

hill, and it is protected by a pine-wood at the back. The view from the front windows looking towards Blackdown, Haslemere, and the Sussex Weald, with the Brighton Downs beyond, is magnificent. "Leybourne," the house built by Mr. Edmund Evans, stands in close proximity to "The Hill," and is similar in style. Its principal feature is a large conservatory or "flower-room" as it was called, fitted up as a sitting-room, where George Eliot, whose strong love for flowers constituted a bond of friendship with its owners, was a frequent visitor. Kate Greenaway, and many other artists, were also wont to assemble there.

CHRISTMAS FESTIVITIES AT "THE HILL"

A VILLAGE INN

SKETCH FOR THE OLD CURIOSITY SHOP

GOING TO MARKET

BURYING THE FAVOURITE

WATERFALL, LOCH ACHRAY

A SURREY COTTAGE

THE DONKEY THAT WOULD NOT GO

COFFEE ROOM OF THE FEATHERS INN, LUDLOW

HONFLEUR.

CHAPTER X

CHRISTMAS FESTIVITIES AT "THE HILL"

SHORTLY after taking up his residence at "The Hill," Birket Foster married, on the 25th of August 1864, his second wife, the daughter of Mr. Dawson Watson of Sedburgh, and a sister of J. D. Watson, a member of the Old Water-Colour Society. Two days previously Foster's niece, Miss Brown, who for many years had had the care of his children, had become the wife of Edmund Evans, and the mistress of "Leybourne."

"The Hill" was an open house to all Birket Foster's friends, and particularly to his brother-artists. He was never more pleased than when he was entertaining his guests, and being specially fond of music, many of the social gatherings were enhanced by musical performances.[1]

One of the most frequent visitors was Frederick Walker, A.R.A.; he was a special favourite, at all times welcome, and was one of the few who had an influence on Birket Foster's painting, especially his figures. He was in the habit of going to Witley whenever he felt inclined without waiting for an invitation, a bedroom known as " Freddy's room " being reserved for him. Walker had an immense love for the place, which he called " Paradise," and greatly regretted that he had not sufficient money to purchase a cottage which J. C. Hook, R.A., had built near his house, the situation of which he considered " romantic—such a sweep of glorious country." In his letters to his sister he referred to his visits to Witley with the greatest rapture. In one he wrote : " To-day here is a fine spring one ; the Downs in the far horizon tinted with gold by the setting sun at this moment. F. and one of the little girls are on the charming lawn playing at

---

[1] He always had a great love for melody, and he used to narrate how, on one occasion when he was sent by *The Illustrated London News* to make a sketch of Jenny Lind whilst she was rehearsing Mendelssohn's " Hear My Prayer " at Exeter Hall, he became so absorbed that he forgot to carry out his commission, and was obliged afterwards to execute it from memory.

bowls, and the birds are going it like mad." And in another letter : " I wish I could tell you how dainty this place is, from the delightful little drawing-room we're now in, with its walls covered with water-colours—little gems by old Hunt, Millais, etc., etc., to the bedroom I occupy and in which I paint, for the subject is the window, which is a large recess, with stained glass and diamond-shaped panes, and I am doing a woman brushing her hair. It is just the house you would revel in, my Poll. Part of the garden is a gentle slope, with its shrubs and bushes covering the beautiful lawn, on which blackbirds promenade in the sun in the morning. There are two smaller flat lawns, on which we play bowls or croquet, and around, down below, planta-tions of firs and pines, and so many evergreens that one forgets that it is the leafless season, and from my bedroom as I sit on the cushions in the recess I can see across to the Brighton Downs and ' Devil's Dyke' thirty miles off." And again in a letter to Mr. Phillips he stated : " I am staying with Birket Foster ever since Sunday week, and shall, I expect, remain a week longer, for I am at work and am happier here than I have been for a long time. . . . This place is the most lovely and snug that I have ever stayed at; all the horrors of

winter and all discomfort of every kind seem done
away with. I can see thirty miles from my bedroom window across the most beautiful part of
Surrey. The house (which B. F. built himself) is
the most perfect: the eye is continually refreshed
by good colour." Walker painted several pictures
whilst staying with the Fosters. In addition to
"The Bedroom Window," to which reference has
already been made, he produced in water-colours
"Two Girls at a Fireside," the two daughters of
Birket Foster, also "The Well-Sinkers," a lady and
little girl looking down a well in course of con-
struction and three labourers standing near, a
subject taken from work actually in progress in
the grounds at the time. The idea for his famous
picture, "The Harbour of Refuge," was first given
to Walker by Birket Foster and Orchardson, who
was staying at "The Hill." One Sunday in church
they noticed a group of bent old labourers on a
long bench, reposing in the gleams of sunlight
that lingered in the gloom of the place. It occurred
to them that it was a subject in which Walker
would delight. He was sent for, and a re-
occurrence of the scene on the following Sunday
took hold of him, and eventually from it "The
Harbour of Refuge" was evolved. Walker had an

idea that there should be a statue of the founder in the picture, and wandered about London in search of one. Meeting Birket Foster one day he exclaimed in an excited manner, " I've got a founder." "Where ?" was the inquiry. " In Soho Square." A statue of King Charles II. formerly stood in the Square. It was removed in 1876, and came into the possession of Mr. F. Goodall, R.A., who re-erected it in the grounds of his house, Graeme's Dyke, Harrow Weald, now the residence of Mr. W. S. Gilbert.

Walker, the "Little Billee" in *Trilby,* was very fond of playing the flute, and frequently assisted in the musical entertainments at Witley. The following is an extract from a characteristic letter to Myles Foster :—

BISHAM, *Aug.* 16/70.

DEAR MYLES—The above being a correct but melancholy representation of the instrument with which in bygone and

21

happier times I was wont to " give breath " (though I may not perhaps—not even when assisted by you on a nobler instru- ment—have " discoursed most eloquent music "), the above, I say, being the sad state into which, through neglect my once cherished flute has fallen. . . . My sister, the companion of my exile, appears to have had a letter from Mrs. B. F. in which she mentions the possibility of a visit from Mr. Jones. Would I were with you !   Shall I launch my frail bark—yea, and wipe the fungous growth from off my flute ? . . . Is there a chance of Mr. Jones and myself once more trying the trio with you ?—Yours disparingly and deboshed,   F.

Another constant visitor was Charles Keene. After Birket Foster had removed from Tig- bourne Cottage he still rented it that he might make sure of the presence of an agreeable and congenial occupant, and persuaded Keene to be- come a tenant.   Keene was greatly delighted with this retreat, of which he wrote to Mrs. Edwin Edwards :

The stillness here after London is delicious.   The only sound is the ring of the village blacksmith's hammer in the distance or the occasional *cluck* of a hen, and the wind roars through the trees of a night, which lulls me pleasantly to sleep.

In another letter he wrote.

This is a pleasant retreat to fly to for a day or two from the row and turmoil of London, and gives my friends too the opportunity of calling it my " country house," and the pleasure of making me wince by hinting at the wealth that

BIRKET FOSTER SKETCHING

Drawn by Charles Keene

enables me to afford such a luxury! It's a bosky-copsy country, very picturesque and English, with just a suggestion (compared to Scotland) of hills on the horizon (the Hog's Back), but from there being so many trees, when the glass does fall the rain comes down with a vengeance. My couch is a hammock, which wraps round me very comfortably, it's like "poppies and mandragora." We have a small aristocracy of artists too down here—Birket Foster, Burton, Watson, and Jones—and amongst our surroundings there is a good deal of fun to be picked up.

The cottage was shared by Keene with another artist, W. H. Hammond Jones. They were an incongruous couple. The former was a regular Bohemian and unconventional, whilst the latter was most punctilious in all little matters of etiquette, and was anxious to shake hands with Keene every morning on his coming downstairs to breakfast, and again before retiring for the night; but Keene resented this little politeness, and endeavoured to prevent it by having his hands engaged by carrying a candlestick, books, or parcels.

When Birket Foster's lease of "Tigbourne" expired, Jones renewed it without consulting Keene, who happened to be abroad at the time. This gave great offence to Keene; he considered that he had been badly treated and never entered the cottage again. He, however, still continued to be a frequent visitor at "The Hill," especially in the month of April, as he was particularly fond of hearing the nightingales. In 1875 he wrote :

I went down to Witley on the 12th purposely to hear the nightingales; they have arrived for the last four years on the 13th at about 11 P.M. This year they did not come on the 15th! and I had to come to town the next morning—a backwardness unknown to the oldest inhabitant.

It became an understood thing that he should go every year to "The Hill" to welcome the first nightingale, and he continued to do so for many years. On 4th April 1886 he wrote :

I hope to run down to Surrey to the B. Fosters about 13th and hear the coming of the nightingales.

Charles Keene was greatly devoted to music. He belonged to several choral societies, and assisted at the festivities at "The Hill" by taking part in glees. The following is an amusing letter written by him when living at 55 Baker Street :—

DEAR MYLES—I send you a "screaming" melody that I've lately become acquainted and am much taken with. It seems to me so quaint and characteristic with all its "tipsy jollity," the way in which the tune never swerves from a sort of timorous dependence on the key-note. I think it very funny. It is very peculiarly "Newcastle," so I want you to keep it to yourself till some evening when your father is quietly at work to play it on the piano and note the effect

on him. I think it must strike on his early recollections and
please him. I hope to be down at Christmas.—Yours very
sincerely,   CHARLES S. KEENE.

Christmas time was a period of much merry-
making at "The Hill," when Birket Foster delighted to collect his friends around him, and a
big house party assembled each year. A description of one of these festive occasions is vividly
given by Keene in a letter to his old friend Edwin
Edwards, written on New Year's Day 1869 : [1]

My joviality has been of a more vulgar character; for
instance, the pleasant sensation of not being very hard at
work after several weeks of " fog," the being in the country,
not seeing any newspapers and with no means of knowing
what day of the week it is, and therewithal the regular
festivities of the season carried on by my friends down here
with an old-fashioned vehemence that carries you away and
fatigues you very effectively. I got down here on the
Monday before Christmas Day, and kept quiet and did a
little work, and on Christmas Eve the guests came in a body
down by the afternoon train, and we all dined at " The Hill "
at six o'clock in the big room.

The fiddle and 'arp came at the same time, and soon after
dinner we set 'em to work, and danced till about three in the
morning, including supper, which is a *sine quâ non* at " The
Hill " whatever time you dine. I had heard from the
Chaplain of the King Edward School that they were going
to sing " Noels " on Christmas morning. The schoolmaster

---

[1] *Life and Letters of Charles Keene*, by G. S. Layard. Sampson Low and Co.

had coached up a quire from among the boys, and I volunteered as a bass, so I was up again at 5.30, and we started at six to sing carols under our friends' windows. Such a sluggard as I may be allowed to boast of this feat. It was pitch dark, so we had to read our parts by the light of our lanterns, and it was very picturesque. The boys, wrapped up in their bed-blankets, were in high spirits, and, ye gods! how they did sing! I shan't forget the sound of those sturdy young trebles in the still morning in a hurry; it was splendid! Everybody was delighted. It was said we were heard a mile off. We had lots of music at "The Hill"; can't say much for the vocal, though we did our best. Little Walker with his flute, and Long Jones with his violin, and another friend of Foster's with his tenor—it was a perpetual "consort of viols." A general tuning was very effective, and then Cooper used to come out with "apples, oranges, ginger-beer, bill of the play"—very excellent fooling; and so it went on, breakfast, lunch, dinner, dancing, supper, and then dancing again; a comic song between whiles, followed by a violin concerto. Cooper was very great. It was very funny, one day, when the three instrumentalists were talking serious shop, he took up the violin and played very slowly and laboriously and out of tune about half a page of the Kreutzer Sonata. On Saturday we all dressed in costume, down to the children, and so to dinner and then dancing again; but now the fiddle and 'arp got the best of us; at twelve o'clock they looked at their watches, pleaded religious scruples, and gave in! Then there was a comparative lull for a few days, broken only by the fitful scrapings of Jones and Walters in some remote apartment. We flared up again last night, and hailed the New Year with the usual ceremonies, and to-day all the guests have departed, and I've come back to my hermitage here; and now leap year is gone, and I'm a bachelor still. . . .

As Keene mentions, one of the amusements at Christmas time was for the whole party to dress up in early costumes. The illustration on the opposite page shows the genial host and a few of his friends in sixteenth-century attire. The two

FALAISE.

fencing are J. D. Watson, in white, and Alfred Cooper, in black; behind the former is Edmund Evans, whilst Birket Foster and W. Lindsay Watson, leaning against the window-sill, are watching the bout. The last named was a nephew of the first Mrs. Birket Foster and a frequent visitor at "The Hill." He died when still a young man, and Fred. Walker, who did not long survive him, thus touchingly refers to him in one of his letters :

Birket Foster and I went for a beautiful walk yesterday morning, finishing up by visiting a little church. In the churchyard they laid poor Lindsay Watson, who first came with the news of my election to the Water-Colour Society, and which I remembered as I stood there yesterday.

22

DRAMATIC PERFORMANCES

PASSING THE FLOCK

THE WEALD OF SURREY

CHILDREN PADDLING

NEAR GODALMING

THE BLACKBERRY GATHERERS

THE PET OF THE COMMON

A SURREY LANDSCAPE

THE HAPPY TIME OF LIFE

TROYES.

CHAPTER XI

DRAMATIC PERFORMANCES

THE Christmas merry-makings at Birket Foster's
hospitable house received fresh zest in 1871 when
it was decided to give dramatic entertainments.
The large open-roofed billiard room was turned
into a picturesque theatre with a good stage at
one end of it. Robert Dudley was invited to take
part in the plays and to act as general manager.
The first performance, " Whitebait at Greenwich,"

173

met with such hearty approval that it was determined to renew these theatricals on a more extended
scale at the next Christmas; and eventually they
became a regular institution for many years.

In the following year Fred. Walker entered
heartily into these "histrionics," or, to quote his
own words: "The Fosters intend to have another
jollification at Christmas, and *entre nous* something
on a complete scale in the *theatrical* line is contem-
plated, into which your humble servant is drifting."
Not only did he paint the scenery for two plays, a
cottage in Lambeth with a view of chimney-pots
seen through a window for "The Birthplace of
Podgers," and a library scene with a fire-place with
pictures hanging over it and book-shelves on either
side most admirably depicted, but he also took the
part of Mr. Erasmus Maresnett, a literary en-
thusiast in the first piece. Walker showed great
power of assuming a character with little aid from
"make-up."

Birket Foster had a strong appreciation of
dramatic art, and he thoroughly delighted in the
preparations incidental to these festivals. There
was something that fell in with his strong kindly
love of old-world hospitalities; he even enjoyed the
rehearsals going on, and worked hard with Walker

at the admirable and varied scenery required in the
pieces.   After one of his sojourns in Venice he
painted a very charming drop scene with a Venetian
view for its subject.

After the Christmas of 1874 Birket Foster was
obliged to obtain help from other artist friends in
the preparation of the scenery, for in the following June Frederick Walker passed away, to the
bitter grief of all at " The Hill," by whom he was
greatly beloved.

These performances lasted for two nights in each
year.   To the first many of the villagers and all
employés of the Fosters were invited.   The replies
to the invitations were sometimes curiously worded
and afforded much amusement to the recipients.
One ran as follows : " The Misses ―― have much
pleasure in accepting Mr. and Mrs. Foster's kind
invitation, and We will be there."   Mr. Dudley
remembers that on one of these first nights, when
it was close upon the time for the performance to
commence, peeping from behind the curtain to see
if the audience were all seated, to his dismay there
was not a single person in the room.   He hastened to
Birket Foster to inquire whether some mistake had
not been made in the date on the invitation card,
and it was suggested that some one should rush off

to the village to find out the cause of the non-arrival of the guests.   He had, however, not far to go, for on opening the hall door a crowd was discovered in the carriage drive.   They were waiting for the doors of the theatre to open!   The writer is indebted to Mr. Dudley for the following list of the plays with the various casts which were acted each Christmas continuously from the year 1871 to 1878.

Characters sustained by

1871. " Whitebait at Greenwich."
- Robert Dudley.
- Myles B. Foster.
- J. D. Watson.
- Mrs. Birket Foster.

1872. "The Birthplace of Podgers." (By J. Hollingshed.)
- R. Dudley.
- A. Cooper.
- Fred. Walker.
- Myles B. Foster.
- Mrs. Birket Foster.

" Fish out of Water."   (By Joseph Lunn.)
- R. Dudley.
- A. Cooper.
- R. Nevill.
- Myles B. Foster.
- Mrs. Birket Foster.

Scenery by Fred. Walker.

1873. "The Jacobite."   (By Douglas Jerrold.)
- R. Dudley.
- A. Cooper.
- Myles B. Foster.
- Mrs. Birket Foster.
- Miss Alice Foster.

" Only a Halfpenny."
- R. Dudley.
- Miss Reeves (Mrs. Horsfall).

Scenery by Fred. Walker and Birket Foster.

Characters sustained by

1874. "A Peculiar Position." (By J. R. Planché.)

- R. Dudley.
- Myles B. Foster.
- A. Cooper.
- Mrs. Birket Foster.
- Miss Alice Foster.

Scenery by Fred. Walker.

"Cool as a Cucumber." (By Blanchard Jerrold.)

- R. Dudley.
- Myles B. Foster.
- Wm. Foster.
- Miss Margaret A. Foster.

Scenery by Birket Foster.

1875. "A Capital Match." (By J. Maddison Morton.)

- R. Dudley.
- A. Cooper.
- Miss Margaret A. Foster.
- Miss Alice Foster.

"Delicate Ground." (By Charles Dance.)

- R. Dudley.
- Myles B. Foster.
- Miss Margaret A. Foster.

Scenery by Birket Foster.

1876. "Our Wife." (By J. Maddison Morton.)

- R. Dudley.
- A. Cooper.
- Miss Margaret A. Foster.
- Miss Ellen Foster.

Scenery—1st Act by Birket Foster; 2nd Act, an old scene by Fred. Walker adapted.

"A Happy Pair." (By S. Theyre Smith.)

- R. Dudley.
- Miss Margaret A. Foster.

Scenery by Birket Foster.

23

Characters sustained by

1877.   " A Blighted Being."   { R. Dudley.
                                       A. Cooper.
                                       Dr. G. Vivian Poore.

        " A Cosy Couple."   { R. Dudley.
                                       Dr. G. V. Poore.
                                       Miss Ellen Foster.

Scenery by Birket Foster.

1878.   " Woodcock's Little Game." { R. Dudley.
                                       Guildford Dudley.
                                       Miss Ellen Foster.

        " Which is Which."   { R. Dudley.
                                       Myles B. Foster.
                                       Miss Ellen Foster.
                                       Miss Alice Foster.

Scenery by Birket Foster.
Also Lecture by Colonel Fogey, F.R.G.S.—Robert Dudley.

Thus these dramatic entertainments were carried with much spirit for eight consecutive years, and at the expiration of that time, much to the regret of Birket Foster and his family, they had to be abandoned. They were only once renewed, namely, on the nights of the 30th and 31st of January 1883, when two plays were acted with the following casts :—

Characters sustained by

" Cut off with a Shilling."   { R. Dudley.
                                       Guildford Dudley.
                                       Miss Ellen Foster.

" Slowtop's Engagements."   { R. Dudley.
                                       Guildford Dudley.
                                       Miss Ellen Foster.
                                       Miss C. M. Chandler
                                         (daughter of the
                                         Vicar).

Scenery by Birket Foster.

As an instance of the generous disposition of Birket Foster, Mr. Dudley tells the following little incident :—After one Christmas dinner, the host, having Mrs. Dudley and Mrs. Nelson, the wife of Captain Nelson, R.N., on either side of him,

CAEN.

cracked two nuts in both of which were double kernels, and gave one to each of the ladies. The next morning there was great excitement on the part of the ladies to say " Bon jour Philippine " to him before he could utter the words. They were both successful in gaining a forfeit from him, but, having received so much hospitality at his hands,

they thought nothing more of the incident.   But
Birket Foster did not forget them; on the following Christmas each lady on her arrival at "The
Hill" found a charming water-colour drawing on
her dressing-table in her bedroom—the forfeits of
the previous year!

LAST YEARS AT WITLEY

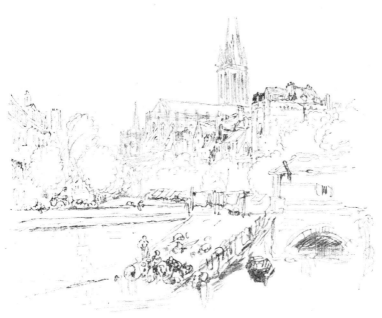

CAEN.

CHAPTER XII

LAST YEARS AT WITLEY

AFTER Birket Foster took up his residence at "The Hill" quite a small coterie of artists and artistic people gathered around him. As we have already seen, Edmund Evans was his neighbour at "Leybourne," whilst Charles Keene and Hammond Jones shared Tigbourne Cottage at the bottom of Wormley Hill. W. P. Burton the water-colour painter lived in another cottage, half-way up it. On the other side of the railway, Birket Foster's elder brother John had a charming residence, "Fernside," with a beautiful garden and grounds running down to the line; the next house, "The Heights," built by Sir Henry Cole, George Eliot purchased with the profits of *Daniel Deronda*, and dwelt for some years, first as Mrs. Lewis and afterwards as Mrs. Cross; beyond was J. C. Hook's residence, "Pine Wood," and at a little distance farther Mrs. Allingham lived at "Sandhills," whilst Kate Greenaway, although not a resident, was a frequent visitor at "Leybourne."

Alas, all has now changed, and what was once the favourite haunt of artists is now deserted by them.

Tigbourne Cottage is now only a gardener's residence attached to Tigbourne Court, a quaint fortress-like edifice. Burton's cottage after his death was rebuilt and has become a modern residence. Here, it may be mentioned, H.R.H. the Princess Louise, Duchess of Argyll, stayed during one summer and honoured the Birket Fosters with a visit.

J. C. Hook left "Pine Wood" because a private retreat was started nearly opposite to his house:

it has been greatly enlarged and is now a country seat of Lord Knutsford, G.C.M.G., whilst Lord Edward Pelham-Clinton occupies "The Heights."

The late Mr. Edgar Horne purchased "The Hill" and resided there. He was a man of considerable taste, and preserved the integrity of the house as far as possible, many of the paintings put up for sale at Christie's in 1894 finding their way back again to "The Hill." The garden was kept in nearly the same state as when Birket Foster used to delight to roam in it, and there still remains a small piece of the ground surrounded by a hedge, with a sun-dial in the middle, bearing the inscription, "Horas non numero nisi serenas MDCCCLXXXIV." This was his special little garden where he was wont to grow wild-flowers. Both Mr. Horne and his wife died within a few weeks of each other at the commencement of the present year, and the property now belongs to her grandson Lieutenant S. B. Boyd-Richardson, R.N.

The Foster family were all fond of the little village of Witley a mile away, where traces of their liberality may be found. Birket Foster, in conjunction with Alfred Cooper, painted the signboard which still swings outside the village inn,

24

"The White Hart." The parish church was restored at the sole cost of Mr. John Foster, who also gave the stained-glass east window, the reredos, and the oak roof to the nave. He likewise erected an Institute in the village at a cost of £2000.

In 1893 Birket Foster was attacked by a serious illness, and yielding to the pressure of medical advice he was obliged to abandon much of his work and reluctantly to give up "The Hill." He removed to "Braeside," Weybridge, where there was a charming garden. Here he continued to reside quietly, devoting himself to his painting as much as possible. At the beginning of 1895 Birket Foster received a congratulatory letter from the Royal Academy of Berlin, on his reaching the age of seventy. It was touchingly expressed, and he was much gratified at its receipt. "Seventy," he said, "used to seem an awful age, but somehow it does not seem so now." In a letter to his old friend Edmund Evans, dated 9th February of the following year, he says: "We are getting old, but with care I hope we may both of us have a few more years to enjoy *this* beautiful world. I have managed with the greatest care to escape as yet catching cold, but it is not *summer* yet. I enjoy my work, I think, more than ever, but

of course I don't do so much as I used to ; I take
my time about it. . . . Herkomer told me he had
been enlarging several of my pictures of English
landscape to illustrate a lecture on composition.
I said to him I thought composition was ignored
nowadays. He said, 'Ah ! it is coming back again.'"
In another letter to Evans, dated 21st February
1898, he refers to a visit to the Winter Exhibition
at the Royal Academy. He says, " I wish you
could have seen the Gilberts—they were really
magnificent. The Millais collection is really a
wonderful one-man show. Though one was
familiar with most of them, they seemed to have
improved ; he was indeed a great painter." He had
also seen the Exhibition at the New Gallery, which,
he adds, "is interesting, but I confess I don't care
for the Rossettis. I thought he was better than
what is shown. Freddy's 'Plough' looks fine,
and I was interested in seeing Millais' celebrated
'Chess-players,' which was painted in an hour or
two, and fetched some thousands of pounds once
at Christie's." Birket Foster finishes this letter in
saying, "You speak of Hastings—they are spoiling
every place ; we have just lived in time. . . . I have
got a bit of a cold, just come on, but I don't think
it is anything. We hope to get away to Torquay at

the end of March, which I shall enjoy.   I am hard
at work completing forty drawings of Scotland for
Tooth, who will exhibit them."

Early in the following year Birket Foster was
taken seriously ill, and died at Weybridge on the
27th March 1899.   In a letter to his daughter two
days later Edmund Evans says : " I feel lonely this
morning, for I went to ' Fernside ' and found Willie
Foster there talking with his uncle about the
funeral of Birket, who died on Monday evening
after three attacks of hæmorrhage following sharp
after each other !   Another link of my chain of life
gone.   I cannot help feeling the loss, for I have
known him since I was fifteen.   He came to
Landells' in his sixteenth year, and we took to
each other at once."   Birket Foster was buried on
1st April on the north side of Witley churchyard.
A Celtic cross, with the simple inscription, " In
memory of Birket Foster.   Born Feb. 4th, 1825.
Died March 27th, 1899," marks the spot where
lie the remains of that great water-colour artist,
who painted English landscape with such a pure
feeling and high perception of the beauty of
Nature.

The artist's eldest son, Myles Birket, as has
already been stated, belongs to the musical pro-

fession, and is a Fellow of the Royal Academy of Music; the second son, William, is following in his father's footsteps as an artist; and the youngest, Henry, is an engineer in the North of

CHURCH OF ST. VINCENT, ROUEN.

England. Of the two daughters, the elder, Margaret Ann, is now Madame Stadnitski, and resides abroad; whilst the younger, Ellen, is the wife of Mr. L. T. Glasson.

It only remains now to add that very shortly after Birket Foster's death his old comrade Edmund

Evans left "Leybourne" and retired to Ventnor. Here he spent his halcyon days basking in the sunshine of that favoured watering-place, often employing his leisure hours in his favourite pursuit of making small water-colour sketches from nature.

This famous colour-printer, to whom so many artists were indebted for the faithful reproductions of their works, passed away on the 21st August 1905 in his eightieth year.

LIST OF THE PRINCIPAL BOOKS
ILLUSTRATED BY BIRKET FOSTER

LIST OF THE PRINCIPAL BOOKS ILLUSTRATED BY BIRKET FOSTER FROM THE TIME HE COMMENCED WORK ON HIS OWN ACCOUNT UNTIL HE CEASED TO DRAW UPON WOOD BLOCKS.

New editions of many of these publications were issued during this period, and numerous wood-engravings appeared in other volumes in subsequent years.

Those marked by an asterisk were entirely illustrated by Birket Foster.

1847

*The Boy's Country Book, in four parts: Spring, Summer, Autumn, and Winter. By Thomas Millar. Chapman and Hall.

1850

Evangeline: a Tale of Acadia. By Henry Wadsworth Longfellow. David Bogue.

1851

*Christmas with the Poets. A collection of Songs, Carols, and descriptive Verses relating to the festival of Christmas from the Anglo-Norman period to the present time, embellished with 50 tinted illustrations. David Bogue.

*The Illustrated Book of Songs for Children. W. Orr and Co.

Voices of the Night and other Poems. By H. W. Longfellow. David Bogue.

The Poetical Works of Oliver Goldsmith. Cundall and Addey.

1852

Poems by H. W. Longfellow, illustrated with upwards of 100 engravings by Birket Foster, Jane E. Benham and others. David Bogue.

*The Story of Mount Blanc and various ascents from the time of De Saussure to the present day. By Albert Smith. David Bogue.

1853

*Hyperion : a Romance by H. W. Longfellow. Nearly 100 engravings. David Bogue.

*Fern Leaves from Fanny's Portfolio. By Fanny Fern (Miss G. P. Willis). 8 illustrations printed with a tint. Ingram, Cooke and Co.

Poetry of the Year. Passages from the poets descriptive of the seasons with 22 chromolithographs. George Bell.

*Visit to the Holy Land, Egypt, and Italy. By Madame Ida Pfeiffer, translated from the German by H. W. Dulcken. 8 tinted illustrations. Ingram, Cooke and Co.

*A Picturesque Guide to the Trossachs, etc. A. and C. Black.

The Lady of the Lake. By Sir Walter Scott. 28 illustrations by Birket Foster, and others by John Gilbert. A. and C. Black.

The Poetical Works of James Thomson. Routledge's British Poets. G. Routledge and Co.

1854

The Lay of the Last Minstrel. By Sir Walter Scott. 44 illustrations by Birket Foster, and others by John Gilbert. A. and C. Black.

*Little Ferns for Fanny's Little Friends. By Fanny Fern (Miss G. P. Willis). With tinted illustrations. Nathaniel Cooke and Co.

Proverbial Philosophy. By Martin Tupper. Hatchards.

An Elegy written in a Country Churchyard. By Thomas Gray. Joseph Cundall.

The Poetical Works of Thomas Gray. Routledge's British Poets. G. Routledge and Co.

The Golden Legend. By H. W. Longfellow. 50 illustrations by Birket Foster and Jane E. Hay. David Bogue.

1855

*L'Allegro and Il Penseroso. By John Milton. *29 etchings on steel.* David Bogue.

Marmion. By Sir Walter Scott. 45 illustrations by Birket Foster, and others by John Gilbert. A. and C. Black.

The Pleasures of Hope. By Thomas Campbell. Sampson Low and Co.

The Poetical Works of Mark Akenside and John Dyer. Routledge's British Poets. G. Routledge and Co.

The Poetical Works of William Cowper. Routledge's British Poets. G. Routledge and Co.

The Task. By William Cowper. James Nisbet and Co.

1856

*The Traveller. By Oliver Goldsmith. *30 etchings on steel.* David Bogue.

*Mia and Charlie. By Harriet Myrtle. David Bogue.

The Poetical Works of George Herbert. James Nisbet.

Sacred Allegories. By the Rev. W. Adams. Rivington and Co.

*Sabbath Bells chimed by the Poets. Coloured illustrations. Bell and Daldy.

Early Lessons. By Maria Edgeworth.

*The Rhine and its Picturesque Scenery. By Henry Mayhew. *20 etchings on steel.* David Bogue.

Willy's Country Visit. By B. Goldfinch.

Songs of the Brave : The Soldier's Dream and other Poems and Odes. By various poets. Sampson Low, Son and Co.

1857

Gertrude of Wyoming. A Poem by Thomas Campbell. G. Routledge · and Co.

The Lord of the Isles. By Sir Walter Scott. 37 illustrations by Birket Foster, and others by John Gilbert. A. and C. Black.

*The Farmer's Boy. By Robert Bloomfield. Sampson Low and Co.

The Rime of the Ancient Mariner. By Samuel T. Coleridge. Sampson Low and Co.

*The Sabbath : Sabbath Walks and other Poems. By James Grahame. Nisbet and Co.

Rhymes and Roundelays in praise of a Country Life. David Bogue.

The Poets of the Nineteenth Century. Selected and edited by Rev. R. A. Willmott. G. Routledge and Co.

The Course of Time : a Poem. By R. Pollok. William Blackwood and Sons.

Ministering Children : a Tale. Seeley Jackson and Halliday.

Poetical Works of Robert Bloomfield. Routledge and Co.

1858

*A Picturesque Guide to the English Lakes. By John Phillips, M.A. A. and C. Black.

*The Grave : a Poem. By Robert Blair. With a preface by Rev. F. W. Farrar, M.A. A. and C. Black.

*The Shipwreck : a Poem. By William Falconer. A. and C. Black.

Kavanagh : a Tale. By H. W. Longfellow. Kent and Co.

The Upper Rhine : the Scenery of its Banks and the Manners of its People. By Henry Mayhew. G. Routledge and Co.

Birds, Bees, and Blossoms. By T. Miller. G. Routledge and Co.

English Country Life. By T. Miller. G. Routledge and Co.

Comus : a Mask. By John Milton. G. Routledge and Co.

Poems and Pictures from Thomas Moore. Longman, Brown, Green and Co.

Pastoral Poems. By William Wordsworth. Sampson Low and Co.

Songs and Poems. By Robert Burns. Bell and Daldy.

The Poetical Works of Edgar Allan Poe. Sampson Low and Co.

Home Affections portrayed by the Poets. Selected by Charles Mackay. G. Routledge and Co.

Lays of the Holy Land : from Ancient and Modern Poets. James Nisbet and Co.

Summer Time in the Country. By R. A. Willmott. G. Routledge and Co.

1859

A Country Book. By W. Howitt. G. Routledge and Co.

The Merrie Days of England. Sketches of the Olden Time. By E. Macdermott. Kent and Co.

*Odes and Sonnets. Illustrations in colour. G. Routledge and Co.

The Hamlet : an Ode, written in Whichwood Forest. By Thomas Warton. *14 etchings on steel.* Sampson Low and Co.

Pastoral Poems. By William Wordsworth. Sampson Low and Co.

The Deserted Cottage. By William Wordsworth. G. Routledge and Co.

The White Doe of Rylstone, or the Fate of the Nortons. By William Wordsworth. Longmans.

Poems. By William Wordsworth. Edited by R. A. Willmott. G. Routledge and Co.

Poetical Works of Thomas Gray. Sampson Low and Co.

Favourite English Poems. Sampson Low and Co.

The Poems of Oliver Goldsmith. Edited by R. A. Willmott. G. Routledge and Co.

1860

The Scottish Reformation : a Historical Sketch. By P. Lorimer, D.D. R. Griffin.

Poems by J. Montgomery. Selected and edited by R. A. Willmott. G. Routledge and Co.

Favourite Modern Ballads. W. Kent and Co.

Merchant of Venice. Shakespeare. Sampson Low and Co.

The Tempest. Shakespeare. Bell and Daldy.

*Common Wayside Flowers. By Thomas Miller. 22 illustrations in colour. G. Routledge and Co.

Lallah Rookh. By Thomas Moore. G. Routledge and Co.

The Carewes. By Margaret Gillies. Kent and Co.

1863

Pictures of English Landscape. 30 engravings by Bros. Dalziel, with pictures in words by Tom Taylor. Routledge, Warne and Routledge.

The following publications were illustrated by means of photography and lithography :—

1867

*Summer Scenes. A series of photographs from some of his choicest water-colours. Bell and Daldy.

1871

*Poems. By Thomas Hood. Illustrations engraved on steel by W. Miller. 2 volumes. E. Moxon, Son and Co.

1878

*Brittany. A series of 35 sketches reproduced by lithography. Published by the artist. The Hill, Witley.

1888

*Some Places of Note in England. A series of 25 drawings reproduced by lithography. Dowdeswell and Dowdsell.

LIST OF WATER-COLOUR PAINTINGS
EXHIBITED AT THE ROYAL SOCIETY
OF PAINTERS IN WATER-COLOURS

LIST OF WATER-COLOUR PAINTINGS EXHIBITED AT THE ROYAL SOCIETY OF PAINTERS IN WATER-COLOURS.

(1) *Summer Exhibitions*

1860 Feeding Ducks.
View in Holmwood Common.
Children going to School.
View on the river Mole.
1861 Wark's Burn, Northumberland.
Gleaners.
Down Hill.
Cattle in Stream.
A Cottage.
Burnham Beeches.
1862 A Lock.
The Bird's Nest.
Fishing.
The Little Nurse.
Water-Lilies.
The Dairy Bridge, Rokeby.
On the Shore, Bonchurch, Isle of Wight.
A Fisherman's Cottage, Isle of Wight.
1863 The Ferry.
A Village Maiden.
Lane Scene, Hambledon.
At Hambledon.
Hay-Carts.
Near Peterborough.
Collier Unloading.
Cottage at Chiddingfold.

River Scene—Evening.
1864 Flying a Kite.
The Donkey Ride.
River Scene.
Cattle Drinking.
Morning.
Evening.
Sunset.
The Wooden Bridge.
Sand-Cart.
1865 On the Beach, Hastings.
Primroses.
The Shrimper.
Expectation.
The Lesson.
The Bird's Nest.
"To gather kingcups," etc.
The Swing.
1866 River Scene—Evening.
Winterbourne, Bonchurch, Isle of Wight.
1867 Bellagio, Lake Como.
The Old Breakwater.
Old Shoreham Bridge.
The Dead Jay.
The Way down the Cliff.
1868 The Mole, near Betchworth.
The Convalescent.
Snowdrops.

The Donkey.
The Little Chickens.
1869 The Meet.
A Breakwater.
A Mill Pool.
Village Children.
A River Scene.
1870 The Weald of Surrey.
Burnham Beeches.
1871 The Valley of the Tyne.
Greta Bridge, Yorkshire.
River Scene with Barges.
On the Thames, Eton.
Rabbits.
Hay Barges.
River Scene with Sheep.
Old Walton Bridge on the
Thames.
Cowslips.
1872 Haymakers.
The Village Inn.
St. Michael's Mount.
1873 Melrose, Dryburgh, Ab-
botsford.
Bereft.
1874 Lausanne, Lake Geneva.
The Spring.
The Return of the Lifeboat.
Antwerp.
Bridge over the Moselle,
Coblenz.
1875 A Cottage.
Fish Stall at Venice.
A Shrine, Venice.
Alsatian Flower-Girl.
1876 A Donkey that wouldn't go.
In the Market at Toulon.
Exercising the Hounds.
Fountain at Toulon.
1877 The Capture of a 32-
pounder.
A Chair Mender.
1878 Venice.
A New Purchase.
1879 The Wandering Minstrels.
The Falls of the Tummel.
1880 Venice from the Guidecca.

West Portal of Rheims
Cathedral.
The Cornfield.
1881 The Stepping-Stones.
An Old Water-Mill.
1882 Turnberry Castle, Ayrshire,
Early home of Robert
Bruce.
The Watering-Place.
1883 A Surrey Landscape.
Clovelly.
1884 A Lane near Dorking.
Passing the Flock.
A Windfall.
An Itinerant Musician.
Gypsies.
1885 The Dipping-Place.
1886 The Hermitage Bridge,
Dunkeld.
Seville.
Sandpits, Hambledon Com-
mon.
Buttercups.
1887 The Lock.
1888 In the Market - Place,
Verona.
1889 Ruined Cottage at Gair-
loch.
A Surrey Lane.
Ben Venue and Ellen's Isle,
Loch Katrine.
A Surrey Farm.
A Cottage on Hambledon
Common.
Cottages at Gairloch, Ross-
shire.
In the Cathedral of S.
Sauveur, Dinan, Brittany.
Washing-Place, near Quim-
per, Brittany.
1890 Arrival of Hop-Pickers,
Farnham.
A Surrey Lane.
Runswick, Yorkshire.
1891 A Knife-Grinder.
Ben Nevis.
In a Garden at Sorrento.

1892   Loch Maree.
The Footpath by the Water Lane.
Oranges and Lemons, Mediterranean.
1893   "To gather kingcups in the yellow mead,
And prink their hair with daisies."
In Glencoe.
Fast Castle, "The Wolf's Crag" of *The Bride of Lammermoor.*
An Old Fiddler.
1894   A Cottage at Taynuilt.
A Market at Seville.
In a Wood, Witley.
In a Garden at Sorrento.
Fisherman's Cottage, North Berwick.
Freshwater Bay.
Near Freshwater, Isle of Wight.
On Hambledon Common.

Cottage at Ballater.
1895   Horning Ferry, Norfolk.
Near Ballater.
Procession on Pardon Day, Quimper, Brittany.
A little Court-yard in the Alhambra.
At Walberswick, Suffolk.
1896   Walberswick.
In a Garden at the Alhambra.
Schrachan, Taynuilt.
A Girl at a Stream.
On Hambledon Common.
Waiting for the Ferry.
Southwold from the Black Quay.
1897   Wild Flowers.
Near Connel Ferry.
Crofters' Cottages at Strath, Gairloch.
1898   Ben Ledi from Callender.
1899   A Milkmaid, Arisaig.

(2) *Winter Exhibitions*

1862-63   Edinburgh Castle.
Studies of Skies.
Studies of Skies.
1863-64   1. At Pinner ; 2. Rocks ; 3. Lobster Pots ; 4. Brighton Boats ; 5. At Bonchurch ; 6. Ryde ; 7. Queensferry ; 8. Rock ; 9. The Spring.
1. Near Littlehampton ; 2. Marsden ; 3. Dunstanboro' ; 4. Newhaven, Firth of Forth ; 5. Queensferry ; 6. At Bonchurch.
1. Craigmillar Castle ; 2. Dunblane ; 3. Craigmillar.

1864-65   1. Hitchin Market Place ; 2. Near Streatley, Haslemere.
1. A Tree Stem ; 2. Preston, Sussex.
1. Streatley ; 2. Richmond Park ; 3. The Ferry ; 4. Barnburgh Castle.
1. River Mole ; 2. River Mole.
1. Old Barn ; 2. On Hampstead Heath ; 3. Saltburn-on-Sea.
Study of Ferns.
1. Ingleton ; 2. Lucerne ; 3. Cottages at Hambledon.

Near Dorking.

1. Ben Lomond ; 2. Near Barnard Castle ; 3. Ben Venue.

1. River Scene; 2. A Barn Roof; 3. Sheep ; 4. Cottages at Chidding-fold : 5. Chiddingfold Church ; 6. The Mill.

1865-66 Four Studies of Village Children.

1866-67 Cottagers.
Trees.
Skies.

1867-68 1. Rocks at Barnard Castle ; 2. Tees' High Force ; 3. Weir at Barnard Castle.

1. At Marsden ; 2. New-biggin by the Sea.

1868-69 Study of Sea, Northum-berland Coast.

1. Study of Hay ; 2. Timber.

A Lock, Stratford-on-Avon.

1. The Peacock ; 2. The Rabbit Hutch.

In the Wood.

Beech Stem—Autumn.

1869-70 1. Grand Canal ; 2. Study of Pots and Girl at a Well, St. Remo ; 3. House on the Grand Canal, Venice.

1. Edinburgh Castle ; 2. Basket of Cowslips ; 3. Barrasford, North Tyne.

Pangbourne.

Autumn Studies.

Richmond, Yorkshire.

1. Loch Lomond ; 2. Creels ; 3. Cottage at Cullercoats.

Haughton Castle, North Tyne.

The Brook at Barrasford.

1870-71 The Greta at Rokeby.
Houses at Eton.
Burnham Beeches.
In the Woods at Burn-ham.
Eton College.

1. Beech Tree ; 2. A Cottage Door.

Eel Pots.

Cottage at Bray.

On the Thames, near Eton.

1. Roses; 2. Nasturtiums.

1871-72 1. Stratford-on-Avon ; 2. Morecambe Bay ; 3. Dunstanboro' ; 4. The Thames at Eton.

The Falls of the Tummel.

Edinburgh.

1. Dead Gull ; 2. The Bass Rock.

1. Newcastle, from Gates-head Fell ; 2. New-castle and the River Tyne.

1. River Bank ; 2. The Punt.

On the Garry.

Cottage at Tarbet.

1. Lancaster ; 2. High-land Cottage, Loch Tummel.

Dunblane.

1. Sunflowers ; 2. Nas-turtiums.

1872-73 St. Andrews.
At Salisbury.

1873-74 Turin.
Study.
Shoreham.
At Verona.
A Fruiterer's Shop.
A Well at Hastings.
Flowers.
Study of Fish.
A Pike.

1874-75 Calais ;   St.   Andrews ;
        Rye.
        Studies of Fish.
        Cologne.
        In a Farmyard.
        On Lake Como.
1875-76 Study of Sea.
        Woodland Scene.
        A Foot-Bridge.
        A Pig Stye.
        On   Hambledon   Com-
        mon.
1876-77 Dunbar Castle.
1877-78 1. Market   at   Dinan ;
        2. Women Washing on
        the Loire.
        Loch Leven.
        In the Church of St.
        Melaine, Morlaix, Brit-
        tany.
        On the Thames at Cavers-
        ham.
        St. Andrews.
        1. Thames   near   Eton ;
        2. On the Stour ; 3.
        The Thames at Ship-
        lake.
1878-79 The Fountain of Drannee,
        Brittany.
        Rouen Cathedral.
        On the Common, Ham-
        bledon.
        A   Sketch   at   Haddon
        Hall.
        Fruit   Stall   near   the
        Rialto, Venice.
        The Letter.
1879-80 On the Coquet at Wark-
        worth.
        The   Thrum,   on   the
        Coquet at Rothbury.
        A North-Country Stile.
        Riverside   near   Wark-
        worth.
1880-81 Cattle in Water.
        On Hambledon Common.
        Stepping-Stones.

Bridge near Dartmouth,
    Devon.
Dittisham on the Dart.
Feeding Geese.
Stream   at   Bedgellert,
    North Wales.
Shelling Peas.
Cottage near Tenby.
1881-82 St. Gervaise, Falaise—
        Market Day.
        Falls of the Tummel,
        Perthshire.
        A Welsh Stile.
        Lyme Regis (two views).
1882-83 An Old Water-Mill.
        Fish and Fruit.
        Lancaster.
        The Brook.
        David   Cox's   Cottage,
        Bettwys-y-Coed.
1883-84 Cottage at Banavie, In-
        verness.
        Highland Bridge, Loch-
        earnhead.
        Ben Nevis.
        The Angler.
        The Kingfisher.
1884-85 In the Western High-
        lands (three draw-
        ings).
        A Surrey Cottage.
1885-86 Ben Venue from Loch
        Achray.
        Highland   Scene   near
        Dalmally.
        A Highland Cottage.
1886-87 Girl at a Brook—Western
        Highlands.
        Loch Awe.
        A Highland Cottage.
        Bridge near Dalmally.
1887-88 Autumn Leaves.
        1. Highland   Cottage
        near   Connel   Ferry ;
        2. In Canty Bay.
        A Spanish Gypsy.
        Cottage at Sidmouth.

Flowers and Fruit (three subjects).
1. Runswick ; 2. Crab and Lobster ; 3. The Old Pier.
A Cottage.
A Farm.

1888-89 A Lacemaker.
1. Abandoned ; 2. Study of Rocks—Gairloch.
1. Study of Rocks ; 2. A Boat—Gairloch.
1. Old Cottages, Hambledon ; 2. Sheep and Lambs.
Crofters' Cottages, Gairloch.
Sketch in Hambledon, Surrey.
Cottage in Talladale, Loch Maree.
A Cottage, Hambledon.
At Gairloch.

1889-90 A Highland Village, Loch Alsh.
Cottage near Balmacara.
Collier unloading.
Haytime.
Harvest-Time — Loch Duich.
A Highland Burn, Balmacara.
Oats, Balmacara.
A Highland Cottage, Loch Alsh.
A Misty Day, Loch Alsh, Ross-shire.
At Balmacara, Skye in the Distance.

1891-92 Fisherman's Cottage, Gairloch.
On the Shore, Gairloch.
Rocks at Gairloch.
Cottages at Gairloch.
Near Loch Etive.
A Fisherman's Garden, Runswick.

A Surrey Lane.
The Sun-Dial.

1892-93 A Highland Stream.
Bridge over the Cluny, Braemar
A Highland Water-Mill.
On Hambledon Common.
On the River Cluny, Braemar.
Near Bonchurch, Isle of Wight.
An Old Mill near Braemar.
A Girl at the Spring.
Cottage near Bonneavie.
Old Pier, St. Andrews.

1893-94 The Model.
Near Braemar.
At Calborne, Isle of Wight.
Barking.
Under the Beech Tree.
Fraser's Bridge, Braemar.
Milton's Cottage, Chalfont St. Giles.
Cottages, Dalmally.
Downey's Cottage, Braemar.
Cottage at Braemar.

1894-95 Cottage at Kimbolton.
A Suffolk Well.
The Stream at Wornditch, Kimbolton.
" June "—In a Cottage near a Wood.
The old Pier, Walberswick.
On the Beach, Southwold.
A Windlass, Southwold.
At Wornditch, Kimbolton.
Walberswick, Suffolk.

1895-96 Near Connel Ferry.
An Orphan.
Butterflies.

The Village Tree.
The Island of Mull from Oban.
Cottages at Taynuilt.
A Highland Cottage.
Cottage near Connel Ferry.
1896-97 On the Canal, Weybridge.
Highland Cottage near Taynuilt.
Burano, Venice.
Loch Etive from near Connel Ferry.
A Farm, Connel Ferry.
Ben Cruachan.
Near Taynuilt.
Roses.
1897-98 A Highland Cottage.

The Alhambra.
A Roadside Shrine near Genoa.
A Rest by the Way.
Haytime.
A Stream.
At Connel Ferry.
1898-99 On the River Spean.
The Pet Lamb.
Roy Bridge, Inverness-shire.
Loch Etive.
Highland Cottage near Taynuilt.
Old Cottages, Loch Etive.
Cottage near Taynuilt.
Cottage near Connel Ferry.

LIST OF OIL PAINTINGS EXHIBITED AT THE ROYAL ACADEMY

1859. A Farm: Arundel Park in the Distance (*Water Colour*).
1869. A Surrey Lane.
1870. Dustanborough Castle.
1871. The Thames near Eton.
The Bass Rock.
1872. Over Sands.
The Ford.
1873. In the Isle of Wight.
A Pedlar.
1874. A Lifeboat: a Return from the Wreck.
The Brook.
1875. On the river Mole—Evening.
1876. A Peep at the Hounds.
1877. A Brook.
1881. The Wandering Minstrel (*Etching*).

persevere

BIRKET FOSTER

INDEX

THE END